Organizing a Speech

Judy L. Haynes

Organizing a Speech
a programmed guide

Second Edition

PRENTICE-HALL, INC.
Englewood Cliffs, New Jersey 07632

Library of Congress Cataloging in Publication Data

Haynes, July L   (date)
   Organizing a speech.

   Includes index.
   1. Oratory.   I. Title.
PN4142.H3 1981   808.5'1   80-29422
ISBN   0-13-641530-X

Editorial production/supervision
      and interior design by *Edith Riker*
Cover design by *Judith A. Matz*
Manufacturing buyer *Edmund W. Leone*

Printed in the United States of America

10   9   8   7   6   5   4   3   2   1

Prentice-Hall International, Inc., *London*
Prentice-Hall of Australia Pty. Limited, *Sydney*
Prentice-Hall of Canada, Ltd., *Toronto*
Prentice-Hall of India Private Limited, *New Delhi*
Prentice-Hall of Japan, Inc., *Tokyo*
Prentice-Hall of Southeast Asia Pte. Ltd., *Singapore*
Whitehall Books Limited, *Wellington, New Zealand*

To my family

as a return on their investment of love.

Contents

Preface

The goal of *Organizing A Speech: A Programmed Guide* is to teach beginning speakers how to organize. To achieve this goal, it combines the best of two methods of instruction: textual narrative and programmed instruction. Each principle of organization is fully explained in textbook style, and then is followed by a series of programmed exercises which give the student practice in applying the principle. As much as possible, the exercises are similar to the kinds of activities speakers engage in as they prepare speeches.

Because this text focuses so intensively on organization, it is not designed to be the sole textbook for a basic course. Instead, it is an ideal supplement for the standard textbook which gives the student an overview of the process of speech preparation and presentation.

The book is designed to be self-instructional, so that other readings or lectures on organization will be unnecessary; but it will be most effective if it is used under teacher supervision. While answers to each exercise are provided, ultimately organization is a creative process, and the student needs feedback on the original product from a teacher, rather than a printed page. To help the teacher measure the student's understanding of the principles practiced in the exercises, each exercise is followed by blanks on which the student indicates whether the answer is correct or incorrect. Most students will be able to evaluate their own responses accurately, while the student who cannot identify his own errors is the one who needs additional help from the teacher.

Chapter 1 explains in detail the concepts covered in this book and offers guides in how to use the book effectively so that all students will achieve the goal of learning how to organize.

The creation of this book involved the efforts of many people and their contributions deserve recognition. The writer is indebted to Larry L. Barker and Robert J. Kibler and their belief that she could write a book on organization. The many student outlines were supplied by Doug Kerr, Fort Steilacoom Community College: Joanne Butler, Tallahassee Community College; and Sarah Lenhart and Thomas R. King, Florida State University.

Judy L. Haynes

1

Introduction

Since we're about to begin the study of organization, the first step is to learn what organization is. The best way to start is to examine some of the related terms and phrases used to describe it, such as *good organization, poor organization,* and *disorganization.*

THE NATURE OF ORGANIZATION

When we say that something has good or poor organization, we imply that organization is a characteristic of a message or system—a characteristic which can be evaluated. The criteria for good organization are that the parts (of the message or system) are related to each other clearly, logically, and efficiently. A filing system is well organized if it is possible to find information easily and rapidly; *a message is well organized if its points are presented in a sequence that its receivers understand without difficulty.*

Two terms, poor organization and disorganization, are used to indicate that the criteria for good organization have not been met. Poor organization and disorganization occur either because no one has tried to organize, or because someone tried but was unsuccessful.

This discussion of organization implies that organization is something which happens (or fails to happen) to a message or system. That is, organization is an active process carried out by the speaker. If it is performed successfully, the process results in good organization; if it is done poorly, it results in poor organization; and if it is not performed, it leaves disorganization. *The goal of this book is to help you produce speeches having the characteristics of good organization.*

THE NEED FOR ORGANIZATION

Learning how to organize is important to the speaker for a number of reasons. The speaker who has taken time to organize will be better prepared and more familiar with his material and therefore will feel more confident while delivering his speech. Confidence, preparation, and good organization usually mean higher grades for the student and more success for any speaker.

No speech will succeed if the audience does not understand what the speaker is trying to say—organization aids the speaker in presenting his ideas in a manner appropriate to the audience. Furthermore, studies have shown that a disorganized message decreases the credibility (the believability) of the speaker for the audience. In turn, lower credibility weakens the impact of the speaker's message. Thus, the speaker who isn't organized has much to lose.

Studying organization can have an additional benefit. Although this book focuses on speech organization, the principles discussed apply equally to preparing themes, papers, and reports. Thus, the student who learns how to organize will acquire a skill which can help in other classes.

THE PROCESS OF SPEECH PREPARATION

Speech organization is one stage of speech preparation. The complete process involves the following steps, often listed in this order:

> PLANNING THE SPEECH
> > Determining the purpose of the speech
> > Analyzing the audience and occasion
> > Selecting and narrowing the subject
>
> BUILDING THE SPEECH
> > Preliminary organization of ideas
> > Gathering material
> > Organizing the material
>
> WORDING THE SPEECH
> > Polishing main points and subpoints
> > Adding oral organization devices
> > Preparing the introduction and conclusion
>
> PRACTICING THE SPEECH

This book concentrates on the steps of speech organization used in building and wording the speech. The steps listed under Planning the Speech and preparing the introduction and conclusion are discussed only as they interact with organization. Therefore, the book is supplementary; if you need a complete overview of the stages in speech preparation, you should consult other sources. **Before beginning Chapter 2, you should be familiar with the steps under Planning the Speech.**

The process of speech organization consists of two phases: *identifying the structure or relationship of ideas* and *arranging the ideas in a logical sequence.* This means that first the speaker must decide what to say (the structure) and then decide in what order to present the ideas (the sequence). The task is much like that of a group of club officers working on the agenda for the next meeting. After they identify all the points they would like to discuss (the structure), they draw up an agenda which lists the items in order of priority (the sequence), so that they discuss the most important matters before the meeting ends.

The majority of this book is devoted to the two phases of structuring and sequencing. Part One provides a short review which covers the rules for preparing outlines, central ideas, and main points. Part Two deals with how to develop the basic structure of the speech; Part Three discusses the sequencing of ideas. Part Four contains a chapter on topics related to delivering an organized speech, such as the preparation of notes; the use of transitions, previews, and summaries; and delivery hints. The final chapter summarizes the steps a speaker should follow in organizing a speech.

HOW TO USE THIS BOOK

As mentioned earlier, the goal of *Organizing A Speech: A Programmed Guide* is to help you with the process of organization. This book is not about organization—it is *how to organize.*

It is a programmed textbook, which is like a workbook because every chapter contains exercises designed to help you practice different organizational skills. The book is designed to be self-instructional. As you go through the exercises, you are your own teacher. It is up to you to decide whether you need to read a certain chapter, whether you understand what is being discussed, and whether your answers are correct. If a chapter contains material you've had before, you have a number of choices—skip the material you're familiar with; skim it quickly for review without doing the exercises; or do it thoroughly.

If the concepts in a chapter are new, take more time with the chapter. Read the text carefully and do all the exercises. If your answers contain many mistakes, you should reread the preceding explanation or go back to a previous chapter which you skipped or skimmed earlier.

Study Guides

To help decide whether you need to study a chapter, each chapter begins with an introduction and a list of behavioral objectives which identify the skills that you will acquire from the chapter. For example, the objectives for

Chapter 2 relate to your ability to follow certain rules in outlining and to identify when an outline breaks the rules. If you know that you don't have the skills identified by the objectives, you may begin the chapter immediately.

As a second guide, each chapter in Part One also has a pretest, since these chapters contain material which may be familiar to you. If you take the pretest and do well, then you have already acquired the skills listed in the objectives. You may either move immediately to the next chapter or skim the chapter for review before going on. *You do not have to take the pretests; do so only if you wish to see if you are qualified to skip a particular chapter.*

If you are in a hurry and know that you will not complete the book, do not begin by working straight through the chapters and quitting whenever your time runs out. The concepts in Parts Two and Three are the most important ones; so, if your time is limited, spend most of it on the chapters in these parts, and either omit or skim Parts One and Four.

Description of Exercises

The outlines used in the exercises were written by beginning speech students, so you may find some outlines which could still be improved. As much as possible, the exercises are similar to the steps to follow in organizing a speech of your own. Some exercises ask you to evaluate outlines in order to help you recognize errors that other speakers have made. In exercises which ask you to identify errors in organization or make other decisions, the correct answer is given immediately following the exercise and is indicated by **Answer.**

In other exercises, you are asked to create original portions of outlines or to explain a situation in your own words. For these exercises, a **Comparison Answer** is given. Your response is not expected to be identical to the comparison answer. Instead, the comparison answer is provided to show you one way to reply to the question and thereby help you to evaluate the correctness of your response.

Example of Exercise Format:

Each exercise is set off by double lines. *Instructions are printed in italics. Work space is provided in the book, directly underneath the instructions.*

Answer: Most answers appear in this half of the page. They are indented immediately under the exercise and are set off by dark lines.

Generally, the number of lines in an exercise does not indicate how many answers you should give. Extra lines are provided to allow enough space for large handwriting.

Since the answer appears directly beneath the question, you should use a piece of paper to cover the answers while you work through the exercise. Some longer answers, such as complete outlines, are placed on a separate, full page. However, they are still set off by lines and are identified at the top as an **Answer** or a **Comparison Answer**.

Underneath the answer are the words *Acceptable* and *Unacceptable,* each followed by a blank. Decide if your answer is acceptable (correct) or unacceptable (incorrect), and then place an X in the appropriate blank. This procedure is to help evaluate your understanding of the chapter. If you have too many X's in the unacceptable blanks, perhaps you need to review the preceding material.

Following are two questions which illustrate the arrangement of exercises and answers. The first question is one having a single correct answer.

Exercise 1.1:

What two phases are involved in the process of speech organization? Write your answer in the space below.

Answer: Identifying the structure or relationship of ideas and arranging the ideas in a logical sequence.

Acceptable _____   Unacceptable _____

The second is an example of a question providing a comparison answer.

Exercise 1.2:

Why should a speaker learn how to organize ideas? List at least two reasons.

> **Comparison Answer:** Organization makes a speech easier to understand; organization is a skill which can be used in other classes for such assignments as writing papers and reports; being organized makes the speaker more confident.

Acceptable _____   Unacceptable _____

SUMMARY

The purpose of *Organizing A Speech: A Programmed Guide* is to teach you how to organize—how to create messages in which the parts are related to each other clearly, logically, and systematically. The emphasis on one stage of speech preparation means that you will have to go to other sources in order to complete your study of public speaking.

This book tries to combine the best of two types of books: the traditional textbook, with its complete explanations of concepts; and the programmed book, with its opportunity for guided practice and its application of principles. Before moving on to Chapter 2, be sure you are familiar with the *Study Guides* discussed on page 3. Remember that *what you learn is up to you.*

part one

review

The chapters in Part One are a review of the skills which are prerequisite to successful organization. *Outlining* is covered in Chapter 2, *The Central Idea* in Chapter 3, and *Main Points* in Chapter 4. Because many students have studied this material in other classes, each chapter is preceded by a pretest. If you pass the pretest, you have the option of skipping the chapter. Remember that the goal is not to skip the chapters, but to learn to organize, so make sure that you really can perform the skills specified in the objectives before moving ahead.

2

Outlining

INTRODUCTION AND OBJECTIVES

All too frequently, *outline* is used as a synonym for *organization,* so that a student assumes his speech is organized because he scrawled an outline with *I*'s and *II*'s and *A*'s and *B*'s. An outline is no guarantee of organization; it is simply a way to display the structure and sequence of ideas so that the organization can be evaluated. The discussion of organization will extend beyond the ability to construct an outline, but all students are expected to have outlining ability before they proceed to the next chapter.

After completing this chapter, you should be able to:

1. Identify errors in outline construction (according to the rules on page 15-16).
2. Revise an outline to eliminate errors.
3. Create speech outlines which do not contain errors.

If you wish to review the rules for outline construction, proceed immediately to page 13 and complete the chapter.

If you have previous experience in outline construction and think you have the skills identified in the objectives, take the following pretest to see if you can skip Chapter 2.

Part I

The followng material was taken from an outline on the subject of gun control. Although the points are in the correct order it no longer looks like an outline.

1. Personal injury and death from gunshots occur more often in the United States than in any other industrial nation in the world.
2. Twenty thousand persons die each year from civilian gunfire.
3. Case of Jean Crez
4. History of the "Saturday Night Special"
5. During the last decade over 900 policemen were killed.
6. The best way to cope with this problem is a handgun-control law which is more clearly defined than the 1968 law.
7. The 1968 Gun Control Act was too narrow in scope.
8. Local and state legislation is too vague, too conflicting, and too inadequate to cope with the problem.

Write the points in correct outline form. Do not change the wording of any of the points.

_____

_____

_____

_____

_____

_____

_____

_____

_____

_____

_____

_____

_____

Write your outline here.

_____

_____

_____

_____

_____

_____

_____

_____

_____

_____

_____

_____

_____

_____

_____

_____

_____

_____

_____

_____

_____

_____

_____

_____

_____

_____

Now go to Part II of the Pretest. Once you have started Part II, do not turn back to this page to make changes in your outline.

Part II

The outline below has several errors. *If there is an error in the entry, circle the entry number.*

1.   I.   The problem is an unknown artifact on Mount Ararat.
2.   A.   What is it?
3.   B.   How did it get there?
4.   II. The problem becomes complex when analyzed.
5.   1.   Location of object
6.   On a 14,000-foot mountain in a glacier 500 miles from the nearest piece of wood.
7.   B.   Size of object
8.   III. There are two possible explanations for the artifact. It may be an idol built by primitives; or it may be the Ark built by Noah.

Scoring the Pretest

To find out how well you did with the "Gun Control" outline, compare your outline with the one on pages 12-13. The two should be identical.
To score your outline:

1.   Add *1* for each symbol that differs from the answer. (For example, if you had an *A* and the correct outline uses a *I,* add *1.*)
2.   Add *1* for each symbol that is not indented the same as the correct outline (for example, "1. Case of Jean Crez" should be indented twice—if yours isn't, add *1*).
3.   For points which took more than one line, such as *I,* add *1* for each continuation line which is not indented parallel with the first word of the point. Add *1* if your answer looks like either of these:

> I. Personal injury . . .
> in the United States
>   or
> I. Personal injury . . .
>   in the United States

Correct "Gun Control" outline

I.   Personal injury and death from gunshots occur more often in the United States than in any other industrial nation in the world.
     A.   Twenty thousand persons die each year from civilian gunfire.
          1.   Case of Jean Cruz
          2.   History of the "Saturday Night Special"
     B.   During the last decade over 900 policemen were killed.

II. The best way to cope with this problem is a handgun-control law which is more clearly defined than the 1968 law.
   A. The 1968 Gun Control Act was too narrow in scope.
   B. Local and state legislation is too vague, too conflicting, and too inadequate to cope with the problem.

Total up the errors on Part I and put the score here. _____

For Part II of the test, you should have circled the following numbers: 2, 3, 5, 6, and 8. Count *1* for each mistake, and place the total here:_____
Now add together the totals from the two sections to indicate how many errors were made on the entire pretest. _____

If your error rate was 0-1, you may skip Chapter 2.

If your error rate was 2-3, you should at least read all explanations carefully, although you do not have to do the exercises.

If your error rate was 4 or more, you should study Chapter 2 carefully, completing all the exercises.

OUTLINE RELATIONSHIPS

Outlining is a technique for representing thought relationships. If all thoughts had equal importance, or if each thought stood alone and had no relationship to any other idea, there would be no need for outlines. However, an outline or some other device which shows relationships is needed for related ideas, such as Popeye, cartoon characters, and Mickey Mouse. We use three common devices to express relationship.

   1. The verbal listing of numbers indicates a series of related thoughts. An example follows.

   "Look, Joe, there are a lot of reasons why you ought to go to a state university. First, there's no out-of-state tuition. Second, . . ."

   2. The visual use of indentation identifies subcategories. An example follows.

   Things to Pack for Trip
      Clothes
         Green Pants
         Swimsuit
      Supplies
         Makeup
         Toothpaste

3. Outlining, which systematically uses both numbers (symbols) and indentation according to a set of specified rules to indicate thought relationships. Thus, the relationships among the education concepts are clearly identified in the following outline:

I. Teacher preparation
    A. Required courses
    B. Student teaching

Outline construction is an important part of speech preparation, as it allows the speaker to check the adequacy with which thoughts have been developed.

KINDS OF OUTLINES

There are three kinds of outlines: *word, phrase,* and *sentence.* The difference between them is the completeness with which thoughts are explained. A word outline provides the least information; the full-sentence outline contains the most. (A word outline is illustrated on page 21, a phrase outline on page 30, and a full-sentence outline on page 25.)

The purpose for which the outline is prepared affects the type of outline that is developed. The initial outline is usually a combination of sentences, phrases, and words. If the speaker is the only one who will see the outline, this may be sufficient. However, if the outline will be read by others, it should contain primarily full sentences so that readers have maximum information about each idea.

A second characteristic of outlines is that they may be either formal or informal. Formal outlines follow strict rules.

1. Every entry (point) is a complete sentence.
2. Every entry begins with a capital letter and ends with a period.
3. Every entry is matched by one or more points of equal importance. If there is an *A,* there must be a *B;* if there is a *1,* there must be a *2.*

Informal outlines bend these rules to fit the specific situation. Most of the outlines used in this book are informal outlines, which means:

1. Main points and subpoints are written as complete sentences,*
    but phrases or words may be used as supporting material.

*Some students' outlines used as examples may violate this rule because they have not been corrected.

2. If there is only one example to support a point, there may be a *1* without a *2*. (This exception applies only to supporting material, not to main points or subpoints.)

Since the requirements for formality in speech outlines vary from one textbook to another, and from one teacher to another, *you should check with your teacher on class standards before preparing any outlines.*

OUTLINE FORM

Whatever the kind of outline, the form remains essentially the same:

I. _____
   A. _____
      1. _____
         a. _____
         b. _____
      2. _____
      3. _____
   B. _____
II. _____

Outline form uses a descending set of symbols in which numbers and letters alternate (*I, A, 1, a*). All symbols of the same rank (for example, *I, II, III*) are placed directly under each other in straight columns, with subordinate (lower) ranks indented equally in a staircase fashion. The number of ranks in an outline will vary according to the complexity of the material, as will the number of items within each rank. Thus, the brief outline on page 14 had only two ranks, whereas outlines for complete speeches will have at least three or four.

RULES FOR OUTLINE CONSTRUCTION

A number of rules govern the construction of outlines:

1. Use a consistent form of symbols and indentation in which numbers and letters are alternated.
2. Assign a symbol to every element of the outline.
3. Make each point a complete thought.
4. Use only one symbol before each point, placing a period after the symbol.
5. Assign only one thought to a symbol.

6. Assign symbols of the same rank to comparable points.
7. Let symbols stand out visually. If a point is longer than one line, indent the second line under the first word instead of beginning under the symbol.
8. Indent less important subpoints under the first word of the more important point. (In typed outlines, each new lower rank is indented four spaces beyond the last rank.)
9. Do not use questions.
10. Capitalize the first word of the point.

The introduction, transitions, and conclusion should not be included in the outline while you are developing the speech. They are part of the finishing touches added in the last stage of speech preparation (see Chapter 10).

To provide practice in recognizing and eliminating mistakes in outline construction, each of the rules is violated one or more times in the following exercises. Identify each error by circling it. Then explain why it is an error in the spaces immediately under the example. Finally, in the next set of spaces, revise the outline to eliminate the errors. The answers are found after each outline.

Exercise 2.1:

Circle all the items with errors in this outline.

I. The common tension headache
    A. Some symptoms of
        a. tension headache
          b. causes of the tension headache
          c. treatment of the tension headache
II. The migraine headache

Explain in writing what the errors are. (Hint: Five rules are violated.) _____

_____

_____

_____

_____

_____

_____

_____

Answer: *A, a, b,* and *c* should be circled. The broken rules are: *1,* letters follow letters; *3,* A is not a complete thought; *6,* comparable ideas are symptoms, causes, and treatment, and they have different levels of symbols; *8,* a, b, c are not indented equally; and *10,* a, b, and c are not capitalized.

Acceptable _____   Unacceptable _____

Place your revision here:

_____

_____

_____

_____

_____

_____

_____

_____

_____

_____

_____

_____

Answer:

   I.   The common tension headache
      A. Symptoms
      B. Causes
      C. Treatment
  II.   The migraine headache

Acceptable _____   Unacceptable _____

Did you remember to compare answers and check either acceptable or unacceptable? If you did not, do so now.

Exericse 2.2:

Circle the errors.

Central Idea: Venereal diseases can be brought under control by education, prevention, and treatment.

  I.   Proper education of people is essential to lessen the epidemic proportions of venereal disease.
     A. What is venereal disease?
     B. What are the early signs and symptoms of venereal disease?
     C. What are the dangers of venereal disease?
 II.   Venereal disease can be prevented.
     A. Proper use of prophylactics is one way it can be prevented.
     B. Cleansing is important in prevention.
III.   Venereal disease can be treated and cured.

Explain in writing what the errors are. (Hint: Two rules are violated.) _____

_____

_____

_____

_____

_____

_____

_____

_____

Answer: The second line of *I* and *A, B,* and *C* under *I* should be circled. Rule 7 is violated, because the second line of *I* begins directly underneath the symbol, rather than being indented. Rule 9 is violated, because *A, B,* and *C* are questions.

Acceptable _____   Unacceptable _____

Explain how you would revise the outline to eliminate the errors: _____

_____

_____

_____

_____

_____

_____

_____

_____

_____

_____

_____

_____

_____

_____

_____

_____

_____

_____

_____

_____

_____

Answer: Indent line 2 beginning with *proportions* so that it is under *Proper.* Revise *A, B,* and *C* under *I* so that they are not questions. A possible revision is:

A. People must know what venereal disease is.
B. People must be able to recognize the early signs and symptoms.
C. People must realize the dangers of venereal disease.

Acceptable _____   Unacceptable _____

The next example contains violations of several of the rules:

Exercise 2.3:

Circle the errors.

"Sneakers"
   I.   Main points
       1. Kinds
       2. Uses
       3. Kinds of people
  II.   1. Kinds
          pointed and rounded toe
          slips-ons and tie-ups
          plaids, ecology signs, racing stripes
       2. Uses

oystering	hiking	jokes
sandlot baseball	photo inspiration	gym class

       3. Kinds of people
          kids
          old ladies
          famous people
 III.   Kinds shown—uses—kinds of people

Describe the errors (five rules): _____

_____

_____

_____

_____

_____

_____

_____

_____

_____

_____

_____

_____

Answer: Every line should be circled. (You were warned that there were lots of errors.) These rules are violated: 1, 2, 4, 5, 7, and 10. There are many errors in symbols, indentation, and capitalization (Rules 1 and 10). One line has two symbols (Rule 4), whereas many lines have no symbols (Rule 2). There are also several examples of multiple ideas to a symbol, such as *III* (Rule 5). The *uses* of sneakers (*2* under *II*) are not indented evenly (Rule 7).

An additional problem is that *I* is the introduction and *III* is the conclusion, which should not be part of the outline.

Acceptable _____   Unacceptable _____

One way to correct this outline would be to revise it like this:

I. Kind of sneakers
    A. Toes
        1. Pointed
        2. Rounded
    B. Fastening
        1. Slip-ons
        2. Tie-ups
    C. Decorations
        1. Plaids
        2. Ecology signs
        3. Racing stripes
II. Uses of sneakers
    A. As footwear for active occasions
        1. Oystering
        2. Sandlot baseball
        3. Hiking
        4. Gym class
    B. As subject for
        1. Jokes
        2. Photographs
III. Kinds of users
    A. Kids
    B. Old ladies
    C. Famous people

SUMMARY

The type of outline that you construct will depend on the purpose for which it will be used. Whatever type of outline you construct it should follow the basic rules on page 15.

3

Central Idea

INTRODUCTION AND OBJECTIVES

The review in the last chapter emphasized the rules of outlining. This chapter contains an overview of what the elements of a speech are (central idea, main points, subpoints, and supporting material) and how these elements fit together. The final section of the chapter is a detailed explanation of central ideas and the rules for preparing them. The other elements are discussed in Chapter 4.

After completing this chapter, you should be able to:

1. Explain the relationship of the central idea to the general and specific purposes of the speech.
2. Explain the relationships of central idea, main points, subpoints, and supporting material with reference to Figure 1 and to outline format.
3. Label the central idea, main points, subpoints, and supporting material in an outline.
4. Identify subordinate and coordinate relationships in an outline.
5. Explain why a central idea is necessary.
6. Revise poor central ideas to follow the rules.
7. Create central ideas which follow the rules.

PRETEST

Take the pretest only if you wish to see if you can skip Chapter 3. Otherwise, go to page 26.

Part I

The numbered items listed below were turned in by students as central ideas for their speeches. However, only a few of the items are acceptable central ideas—the rest need considerable revision. *Place an X in the blank beside each central idea which needs revision.*

_____ 1. To relate to the audience the existence of chemical weapons, the history of their use, and their moral implications.

_____ 2. There are three Greek words for love, and all three types of love are needed in a marriage.

_____ 3. How Mickey Mouse came into being.

_____ 4. The turning point of the Civil War was the Battle of Gettysburg.

_____ 5. To inform the audience about dreams.

_____ 6. I'm going to talk about the metric system.

_____ 7. What stress can do to you.

_____ 8. Some of the food additives you consume may have harmful effects.

_____ 9. To convince the audience of the need for atomic breeder reactors as power generators.

_____ 10. There are three reasons why Aberdeen Angus cattle are the best breed.

_____ 11. The Dead Sea Scrolls.

_____ 12. The philosophy and highlights of new material on health education, which will be presented in two parts.

Part II

Several terms are used to describe the relationship of ideas. This section will test your ability to identify the relationships and use the terms. *Look at the outline, and then choose the appropriate term to make each of the statements below descriptive of the outline.* Your choices are:

a. Coordinate with
b. Superordinate to
c. Subordinate to
d. Not related to

1   I. We must act immediately to bring our population under control.
2   A. A system of financial rewards and penalties needs to be legislated.
3   1. We need to reverse our income tax encouragement of reproduction.
4   2. We need to reward voluntary sterilization.
5   3. We need to make adoption procedures simple.
6   4. We need to put a luxury tax on baby items.
7   B. Sex education must be mandatory in all schools.
8   1. The "birds-and-the-bees" approach should be eliminated.
9   2. Sex should not be defined as a reproductive function.
10   C. Population-related research must be expanded.
11   1. Effective contraceptive methods should be found.
12   2. Human sex determination should be researched.
13 II. We must act immediately to eliminate deleterious effects on our environment.
14   A. Industrial and automotive air pollution must be eliminated.
15   B. Pesticide pollution of air and other parts of our environment must be eliminated.
16   C. Industrial and sewage pollution of waterways must be eliminated.

The questions about the outline will be of the form: *I*, line 1, is _____*A*, line 2. *Decide which of the four terms (a, b, c, or d) would best fill in the blank to make the statement true, and put the appropriate letter in the blank.*

13. *I*, line 1, is _____*C*, line 10.
14. *B*, line 7, is _____*1*, line 8.
15. *B*, line 15, is _____*II*, line 13.
16. *A*, line 2, is _____*C*, line 16.
17. *3*, line 5, is _____*4*, line 6.
18. *1*, line 8, is _____*A*, line 2.
19. *I*, line 1, is _____*2*, line 9.
20. *4*, line 6, is _____*I*, line 1.

Scoring the Pretest

For Part I, you should have X's in front of 1, 3, 5, 6, 7, 9, 11, and 12. The rest of the items are acceptable central ideas.

The answers for Part II are:

13. b
14. b
15. c
16. d
17. a
18. d
19. b
20. c

Now add up the total number you missed, and place the total here: _____

If you missed no more than one in each part, read pages 26-29, and then skip the remainder of Chapter 3.

If you missed three, read all explanations carefully, although you do not have to do the exercises.

If you missed four or more, study Chapter 3 carefully, completing all of the exercises.

SELECTION OF TOPIC, SPECIFIC PURPOSE, AND CENTRAL IDEA

The initial stages of speech preparation involve selecting a topic and a speech purpose. In a speech class, the general purpose of your speech, such as to inform, persuade, or entertain, is usually assigned. This limitation happens in real-life speaking situations too, when the situation dictates the purpose and often the topic you select. For example, your history teacher requires an informative oral report chosen from a list of subjects, or a church group asks you to give a speech to convince or persuade them on a topic related to religious principles. In other situations, you will be free to select both your general purpose and topic.

Specific Purpose

Once you have chosen the topic and general purpose, you must identify your specific purpose for giving the speech. The specific purpose ties together the topic and the general purpose of the speech. *The specific purpose is the response you wish from the audience.* If you are running for a student-body office, your general purpose is to persuade; your specific purpose is to obtain votes. In an informative speech, your specific purpose may be to have the audience learn how to select high-quality fresh fruits and vegetables.

Central Idea

The specific purpose is closely related to the central idea of the speech. *The central idea—often called the theme, thesis, or purpose statement— is the concept that the speaker wants the audience to remember or to practice. The central idea states or implies the specific response desired of the listeners.* For example, the central idea of a campaign speech might be that "Jonah is the best man for the job, so you should vote for him." Other examples of specific purposes and central ideas are:

1. *Specific Purpose:* to convince the audience to use organic gardening.
    Central Idea: There are three reasons why organic gardening is the best type of gardening.
2. *Specific Purpose:* to acquaint the audience with the values and uses of the dictionary.
    Central Idea: The dictionary is a valuable tool.
3. *Specific Purpose:* to entertain the audience by showing them different uses for whipped cream.
    Central Idea: Whipped cream is a fine toilet article and personal article.

Exercise 3.1:

In the following example, does the central idea reflect the specific purpose of the speech?

Specific purpose: to convince the audience that everyone needs more physical exercise.
Central idea: Exercise is good for the heart.

Explain why the central idea does or does not adequately reflect the specific purpose.

_____

_____

_____

Answer: The central idea is inadequate because the specific purpose is to convince, whereas the central idea is to inform. The central idea should be expanded to cover other reasons besides helping the heart.

Acceptable _____   Unacceptable _____

RELATIONSHIP BETWEEN CENTRAL IDEA AND SPEECH CONTENT

The central idea controls the ideas presented in a speech. Thus, building a speech is like building a pyramid; everything in the speech (the base) must support the central idea (the top). Figure 1 shows the pyramid structure of an organized speech.

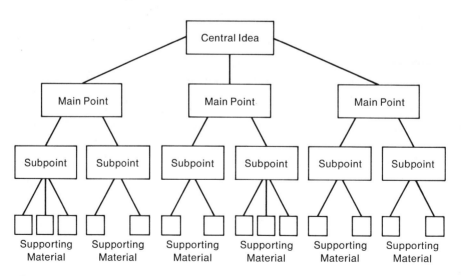

Figure 1. Representation of Pyramid Structure of Speech Organization (Theodore Clevenger, Jr., and Jack Matthews, *The Speech Communication Process.* Glenview, Illinois: Scott, Foresman and Company, 1971, p. 99.)

As Figure 1 illustrates, the supporting materials (examples, details, statistics, quotations) reinforce the subpoints. In turn, the subpoints back up each main point, and the main points develop the central idea. This figure shows only one level of subpoints, but complex speeches may have two or three levels of subpoints. Figure 3, page 61, is an example of the pyramid structure.

Content Units

Each main point, with its subpoints and supporting materials, forms a *content unit.* Most speeches have between two and five content units. The model in Figure 1 has three content units, since it has three main points. The content units form the *structure* of the speech. Structure refers to the building blocks (the content units) that will be assembled in some sequence to create the speech.

Speech structure and the model in Figure 1 are closely related to the speech outline. In an outline, as in Figure 1, the main point, its subpoints, and the supporting material form a content unit. The central idea and the specific purpose are not part of the outline, but precede it, as shown in the "diabetes" outline (page 30). The outline begins with the main points, which received the Roman numerals *I, II, III,* and so on. Each main point is supported by two or more subpoints (*A, B, C*), which in turn are subdivided into supporting material or details (*1, 2, 3,* and *a, b, c*).

Here is some practice in identifying the different elements of a speech.

Exercise 3.2:

How many content units does the diabetes outline have?

_____

_____

_____

_____

_____

Answer: Three, each headed by a main point (identified by the Roman numerals I, II, III).

Acceptable _____   Unacceptable _____

Identifying Possible Diabetics*

Specific Purpose: to inform students that they may be hidden diabetics.
Central Idea: If you know the factors which lead to diabetes and its symptoms, you can decide if you need to be tested for diabetes.

I.   Although the actual cause of diabetes is not known, scientists have found certain factors which are related to diabetes.
    A. People over forty (women especially)
    B. Overweight people
    C. People related to diabetics
    D. Women who have shown carbohydrate intolerance during pregnancy
    E. Women who have given birth to large babies (9 lbs.)
II. Knowing the symptoms of diabetes can help you decide if you have the disease.
    A. Symptoms
        1. Frequent urination
        2. Abnormal thirst
        3. Rapid weight loss
        4. Extreme hunger
        5. Drowsiness (may be only symptom)
        6. General weakness
        7. Visual disturbance
        8. Skin infections
        9. Mental disturbance
    B. Example of woman who had some of the symptoms
III. Doctors have several tests by which they can diagnose even mild cases.
    A. Types of tests
        1. Urine test
        2. Blood test
        3. Glucose-tolerance test
    B. Frequency of testing
        1. At least once a year

What are the subpoints under the third main point?

_____

_____

Answer: *A.* Types of tests and *B.* Frequency of testing.

Acceptable _____   Unacceptable_____

*Janis Turner, speech material prepared at Tallahassee Community College (unpublished) 1972.

Terms for Relationships

Three terms are used to describe the relationships which exist between the various elements of an outline. Since these concepts will be used throughout the book, you should master them now.

1. **Every element is coordinate with one or more other elements.** Coordinate elements represent the same level of generalization, abstraction, or importance; and they are equal, similar divisions of the same classification. Examples of coordinate items are "Pinto," "Mustang," and "Fairmont" (cars made by Ford); elementary, junior high, and high school (levels of education); and willingness to give, honesty, and sensitivity (characteristics which people should develop before marriage).

In Figure 1 items in the same row (across) which are connected to a common higher-level point are coordinate. In an outline, coordinate ideas are indented equally and have symbols of the same rank. In the sample outline on diabetes, the factors listed under I (A through E) are coordinate.

Exercise 3.3:

Look at the diabetes outline and decide if the following statements about coordinate elements are true or false. Circle the correct response.

T   F   *I, II,* and *III* are coordinate.

Answer: True. The main points are coordinate.

Acceptable _____   Unacceptable _____

T   F   *I* and *A* are coordinate.

Answer: False. The main points and the subpoints are not coordinate.

Acceptable _____   Unacceptable _____

T F   *1, 2,* and *3* under *III A* are coordinate.

Answer: True. Supporting materials or subpoints which belong to the same content unit (see Figure 1) are coordinate.

Acceptable _____   Unacceptable _____

T F   The central idea is coordinate with *I, II,* and *III.*

Answer: False. The central idea includes all the main points.

Acceptable _____   Unacceptable _____

2. **Most elements also belong to one or more superordinate/subordinate relationships, in which the elements are related but are not of equal importance or generalization.** Subordinate elements support the superordinate, more abstract concept. For one example, "Pinto" is subordinate to "cars made by Ford"; and "elementary school" is subordinate to "levels of education."

In outlines, subordinate elements are indented to the right of the superordinate element. In the diabetes outline the factors *A-E* are subordinate to *I,* since they are divisions of the term *factors.* Conversely, *I* is superordinate to the factors *A-E.*

Exercise 3.4:

Fill in each blank with the correct element from the diabetes outline.

A. *Symptoms* is subordinate to _____.

Answer: *II. Knowing the symptoms. . .*

Acceptable _____   Unacceptable _____

A. *Symptoms* is superordinate to _____.

Answer: *1—9.*

Acceptable _____   Unacceptable _____

A. *Symptoms* is coordinate with _____.

Answer: *B. Example of woman . . .*

Acceptable _____   Unacceptable _____

Exercise 3.5:

Fill in the blank with the correct term.

1. The central idea is superordinate to the_____.

Answer: Main points (and to the rest of the speech).

Acceptable_____   Unacceptable _____

2. The subpoints are subordinate to the _____.

Answer: Main points.

Acceptable _____   Unacceptable _____

3. The subpoints are superordinate to the _____.

Answer: Supporting material.

Acceptable _____   Unacceptable _____

====

3. **The terms coordinate, superordinate, and subordinate cannot be applied to elements which are not related to each other.** For example, *B. Example of woman* and *A. Types of tests* are not coordinate, even though they have the same order symbols and are indented equally, because they are subordinate to different ideas. In a model like Figure 1, they are on the same row but are connected to different main points.

====

Exercise 3.6:

Decide whether the following statements about relationships in the diabetes outline are true or false. Circle the correct response.

T   F   *A. Types of tests* is subordinate to *II*.

Answer: False. *A* is subordinate to *III. Doctors have . . .*

Acceptable _____   Unacceptable _____

T   F   *1. Frequent urination* and *2. Blood test* are coordinate.

Answer: False. They are supporting material for different subpoints.

Acceptable _____   Unacceptable _____

T   F   *9. Mental disturbance* is subordinate to *II*.

Answer: True. If you said false out of habit, think again. *9*, a symptom, is related to *II. Knowing the symptoms.*

Acceptable _____   Unacceptable _____

THE ROLE OF THE CENTRAL IDEA

The central idea is a precise statement which reflects the specific purpose and the content of the speech. It is superordinate to the content units (the main points, subpoints, and supporting material) used to develop the speech.

Although stating the central idea may seem an unnecessary exercise, many speeches fail precisely because the speaker failed to identify what he really intended to put in the speech. Stating your central idea clearly will save time and effort in the other steps of preparation. By stating the central idea, you will have limited the subject and determined what should be in the speech, which will reduce research time. A clear statement of the central idea will also minimize the amount of time spent in structuring the speech and sequencing ideas.

Identifying the central idea will not always be easy, particularly in informative speaking where you wish to speak *about* something and are less specific about a desired response from the audience. And it's not a "do it once and then forget it" task. Although you should draft your central idea before doing research, you may have to modify it after you've looked at the information available, and you may need to revise it again after you fit your speech to the amount of time available.

In summary, *the central idea is the controlling thought in the speech.* Everything else should be subordinate and related to that idea, just as Figure 1 shows. For many speeches, the central idea will be the one point which the speaker most wants the audience to remember. Whether or not the speaker ever specifically states the central idea, he should begin preparing a speech with at least a preliminary attempt at identifying the controlling thought.

RULES FOR WRITING CENTRAL IDEAS

The rules and examples which follow represent the ideal in stating your central idea. Since you may be unable to produce such specific statements during your initial organizational efforts, you may need to modify your original central idea as you move through the stages of speech development.

1. A central idea should reflect the specific purpose of the speech. The reasons for this rule and some good examples were given on page 27.

Exercise 3.7:

Rewrite the central idea in Exercise 3.1 on page 27 to reflect the specific purpose.

Comparison Answer: (Remember that your answer isn't expected to be a word-for-word replica of this answer.)
Everyone needs more exercise.

Acceptable _____   Unacceptable _____

2. **A central idea states specifically what will be discussed in the speech.** In doing so, it limits the subject area, thereby simplifying research. This rule particularly applies to central ideas for informative speeches.

Exercise 3.8:

Which of these statements identifies specifically what will be discussed in a speech? Circle the answer.

1. Rising food costs.
2. I'm going to discuss rising food costs.
3. Farmers are not to blame for the rising cost of food.

Answer: *3* should be circled, since it limits the subject to a specific area of the problem. The other two items simply identify the general subject.

Acceptable _____   Unacceptable _____

Exercise 3.9:

For a speech describing the development of flying machines up to 1903, which would be the better central idea? Circle the number.

1. The history of flying is interesting.
2. Throughout the ages, man has attempted to develop flying machines.

Answer: *2,* since it outlines the contents of the speech and is more specific than *1.*

Acceptable _____   Unacceptable _____

As this example demonstrates, the use of adjectives like *interesting* does not add specificity to a central idea. You should substitute a concrete description of exactly what you're going to discuss.

Exercise 3.10:

Which is a better central idea? Circle the number.

1. Rome is one of the most popular attractions in the world because of its history, its beauty, and its religious importance.
2. Rome is beautiful.

Answer: *1* is better, since it is a central idea which identifies the content.

Acceptable _____   Unacceptable _____

3. **The central idea should be a clear, concise sentence.** Sometimes speakers do not follow this rule, so they come up with very awkward sentences or phrases. The central idea should state clearly what the speech will cover.

Exercise 3.11:

Here are some central ideas which beginning speech students wrote. Revise them to make them complete, clear sentences.

1. Smoking a pipe—four pieces of advice for beginners.

_____

_____

_____

Comparison Answer: Someone who is just beginning to smoke a pipe should know four things. Or: A beginning pipe smoker must learn how to do four things.

Acceptable _____   Unacceptable _____

2. To convince the audience that knowledge of automotive engines can be of benefit by presenting two reasons.

_____

_____

_____

Comparison Answer: Knowing how your car's engine works can benefit you in two ways.

Acceptable _____   Unacceptable _____

3. A college education secures three advantages to the student.

_____

_____

_____

Comparison Answer: A college education gives students three advantages over nongraduates.

Acceptable _____   Unacceptable _____

4. To acquaint the audience with a few of the people and feats they were first in doing something pertaining to aviation.

_____

_____

_____

Comparison Answer. We should learn about some of the people who made aviation firsts.

Acceptable _____   Unacceptable _____

SUMMARY

When preparing a speech, you typically begin at the top of the pyramid; that is, you identify the topic and the general and specific purposes of the speech and then write the central idea. A central idea should reflect the specific purpose of the speech; state specifically what will be discussed; and should be a clear, concise sentence.

Once you have identified the central idea, you can begin the research stage, since you now have a guide to assist in identifying relevant material. The next step (whether it is done before, during, or after the research stage) is identifying the main points and subpoints of the speech. The rules for the preparation of these elements are given in the next chapter.

4

Main Points

INTRODUCTION AND OBJECTIVES

In Chapter 3, you studied the relationship between the general and specific purposes, the central idea, and the content units, in terms of Figure 1 and in terms of outline format. You also received an introduction to the rules for preparing central ideas.

This chapter continues the discussion of the concepts in Chapter 3. Chapter 4 is a detailed study of the key elements of an outline—the main points and subpoints—and the rules guiding their construction.* The emphasis in this chapter is on recognizing and eliminating common errors, while the process of creating main points and subpoints is studied in Parts II and III.

After completing this chapter, you should be able to:

1. Identify main points which violate the rules given in this chapter.
2. Revise main points to eliminate errors.
3. Create main points which do not contain errors.
4. Apply the rules in developing subpoints.

---

*Supporting material, the third component of a content unit, is not a topic discussed in this textbook. For information on types of supporting materials and how to use them see Alan H. Monroe and Douglas Ehninger, *Principles and Types of Speech,* 8th ed. (Glenview, Ill.: Scott, Foresman & Co., 1978).

PRETEST

Take the pretest only if you wish to see if you can skip Chapter 4. Otherwise, go to page 44.

Part I

Each central idea is followed by several main points. All main points in a set may be correct, or there may be one or more main points which should be omitted or revised because they are constructed poorly or do not support the central idea. *Circle the symbol of each main point which should be omitted or revised.*

Set 1

Central Idea: There are several things that you can do to prepare yourself to vote intelligently.

I. Keep up with current events so you can evaluate what candidates say about them.
II. Follow the campaign closely, through all available media.
III. Campaign for the candidate of your choice.
IV. Keep track of the voting records of each incumbent so you'll know what each has done.

Set 2

Central Idea: Society, not genetic factors, causes most of the personality differences between males and females.

I. Sex differences are caused by the differences in physical objects and surroundings traditionally assigned to males and females.
II. They are caused by the activities traditionally performed by each sex.
III. They are caused by the personality expectations for males and females.

Set 3

Central Idea: The person who wants to maintain his present weight or lose weight should know these facts.

I. Avoid miracle, super-quick diets, because the weight loss is usually temporary, and because they may make you sick.

II. Doing more exercise can help you maintain or lose weight.

III. Re-evaluation of eating habits to discover where you consume unnecessary calories.

IV. Knowing the caloric value of foods can help you substitute less fattening foods.

Part II

A central idea is given below. Following the central idea are four sets of main points. Choose the four best main points, one from each set, to support the central idea. *Circle the number of the best main point in each set.*

Central Idea: Society, not genetic factors, causes most of the personality differences between men and women.

Set 4

1. Different treatments for babies, depending on sex.
2. People react to girls and boys in different ways; they prepare different surroundings and play things; and they dress them differently.
3. From the day they are born, baby girls and baby boys are treated differently.

Set 5

1. Children are raised according to supposed sex differences.
2. Girls and boys are expected to choose different recreational activities.
3. Discrimination begins the day the child leaves the hospital and continues through childhood.

Set 6

1. Dating and job expectations confirm sex differences.
2. Teenage experiences perpetuate the sex-difference myths.
3. The roles for marriage partners are based on sex differences.

Set 7

1. Sex-difference patterns force men and women into traditional marital roles.
2. Adults are expected to behave according to preconceived sex roles.
3. Stereotypes of behavior, based on supposed sex differences, are even expected of the elderly.

Scoring the Pretest

In Set 1, *III* should be circled. In Set 2, there are no errors. In Set 3, *I* and *III* should be circled. The answer for Set 4 is *3;* for Set 5, *1;* for Set 6, *2;* for Set 7, *2.* Count up your errors and place the total here: _____.

If you missed 0-1, you can apply the rules covered in Chapter 4. Before going on to Chapter 5, scan Chapter 4 for a quick review of the rules (given in boldface type).

If you made 2-3 errors, you should read all explanatory materials (the text). Do the exercises if you wish additional practice.

If you missed more than 3, study the chapter carefully, completing all exercises.

THE ROLE OF MAIN POINTS

Although any message has only one central idea, it usually consists of a number of main points. If a member of the audience were asked after a speech what the speaker had said, he would respond—we would hope—with the central idea. If asked why that central idea is true, he should respond with the main points.

The *main points identify the major divisions of the body of the speech* (in this discussion, the introduction and conclusion are not included as main points). A speech about Renaissance art might be divided into main points dealing with the different art forms or with the countries which produced the masterpieces. In a speech describing the steps used in printing a newspaper, the main points could be the major steps in the process.

In a persuasive speech, the main points are the supports or reasons (the major ones) for accepting or believing the central idea. For example, in a persuasive speech advocating increased salaries for public school teachers, the main points might be a description of the need for higher salaries, an explanation of where the money will come from, and a discussion of the advantages of higher salaries to the taxpayer.

For any speech, *the number of main points should be limited. Five generally is considered the maximum number, while most speeches have at least two.* The reason for the limitation is consideration for the audience. Main points are designed to be remembered, and there is a limit to the number of points people can absorb in one sitting. Occasionally, for very short speeches, there may be only a central idea, but such speeches are rare.*

---

*These are usually called one-point speeches. Common forms of the one-point speech are the acceptance speech or the brief inspirational talk, which consists of a couple of examples and a conclusion.

RULES FOR WRITING MAIN POINTS

The rules for writing main points are related to the rules for outlines in Chapter 2, but these rules concentrate on the content rather than on the form of the outline. They are also specifically tailored to the needs of public speaking, rather than to general outline preparation. Since the rules apply equally well to the preparation of subpoints, whenever the term *main points* appears, add *and subpoints*.

   1. **When preparing a speech outline, write each main point as a single, complete sentence, so that you can test the adequacy of your thought development.** If you do not know what a complete sentence is, ask an English teacher for assistance. No practice will be given in identifying complete sentences, though you may refer back to the brief discussion on page 14.

Exercise 4.1:

One student tried to crowd too many sentences into a main point. Underline the one sentence which would serve as an adequate main point for his ideas.

I. There was really no reason for the battle at Gettysburg. Neither side was ready to fight. There were several factors that contributed to the battle, even though neither army was ready to fight.

Answer: The third sentence should be underlined, since it sums up the ideas contained in the other two.

Acceptable _____   Unacceptable _____

---

   2. **Each main point must contain only one major idea.** If a proposed main point contains two major ideas, you should separate them and write them as two different points.

Exercise 4.2:

Determine whether each of the following is or is not an adequate main point by circling the correct response.

1. Group discussion encourages participation from all members.

   Adequate   **Inadequate**

   _____

   Answer: Adequate. The main point contains only one major idea.

   _____

   Acceptable _____   Unacceptable _____

2. Drunken driving is increasing and should be punished more severely.

   Adequate   **Inadequate**

   _____

   Answer: Inadequate. The main point has two major ideas: the increase of crime and the punishment of violators. It should be separated into two main points.

   _____

   Acceptable _____   Unacceptable _____

3. Since the amount of drunken driving is increasing, we should have stricter laws against it.

   Adequate   **Inadequate**

   _____

   Answer: Inadequate. Even though the main point is a reworded version of the previous example, it still contains the same two ideas.

   _____

   Acceptable _____   Unacceptable _____

4. This school has a serious problem with parking.

   Adequate   **Inadequate**

   _____

   Answer: Adequate.

   _____

   Acceptable _____   Unacceptable _____

Exercise 4.3:

Here is an inadequate main point. See if you can write it as two separate points.

Cheating on tests and violating housing rules should be punished more severely.

I. _____

_____

II. _____

_____

Comparison Answer:
I. Cheating on tests should be punished more severely.
II. Violating housing rules should be punished more severely.

Acceptable _____   Unacceptable _____

Exercise 4.4:

A student came up with one very complex main point for his speech. Can you revise it so that what he is trying to say becomes a little clearer?

Taking the heart as a muscle and explaining the effects of exercise on the heart as a muscle and why there is a need for exercise.

_____

_____

_____

_____

Comparison Answer:
I. Exercise affects the heart in a number of ways.
II. The heart needs exercise for several reasons.

Acceptable _____   Unacceptable _____

3. **Main points should be approximately equal in importance.** More will be said on this subject in Chapters 5, 6, and 7, but for now here is an example. In a speech on political parties in the U.S., rather than having ten or twelve main points for all of the parties that have appeared, you might discuss each major party separately, while you combine the minor parties under one main point, as:

I. The Republican Party is the oldest of the existing parties.
II. The Democratic Party is the second major party.
III. Minority parties have been influential at various times in the history of the U.S.

Exercise 4.5:

How could you discuss the possible side effects of the oral contraceptive ("The Pill") without making a long list?

Answer: Treat the major effects as separate points, and lump the minor ones together under one heading:
  I. One of the most serious effects . . .
  II. A second important effect . . .
  III. Other possible effects . . .

Acceptable _____   Unacceptable _____

---

4. **Main points should not overlap, and they should not leave gaps in the material covered by the central idea;** that is, they should be mutually exclusive, yet all inclusive. If you were discussing major land masses of the world, you would not discuss Africa twice under different headings, nor would you omit it. *In some cases, overlapping is caused by the speaker's failure to see that what he lists as two separate points are almost identical and may be combined.*

Exercise 4.6:

Can you find the overlap in this example?

   I.   Reasons for superstition
      A. Desire to appease fate and to invite fortune
      B. Avoid the evils man could not understand
      C. Pry into the future
  II. Bases why superstition existed
      A. Ignorance
      B. Fear
 III. Examples of superstition

Which points overlap? _____

_____

_____

_____

_____

_____

_____

_____

_____

_____

_____

_____

_____

Answer: *I* and *II* are almost identical.

Acceptable _____   Unacceptable _____

     In other cases, overlapping occurs when one of the main points is actually a subpoint. In that case, one of the items should be rewritten (if needed) and indented under the appropriate main point.

Exercise 4.7:

How may this outline be revised to eliminate overlapping main points? (Tell how; don't rewrite the outline.)

Central idea: All students should live in an on-campus dormitory during their freshman year.

  I.   Freshmen need the social life offered by the dorm.
 II.   Freshmen need the supervision offered by dorm parents and counselors.
III.   Freshmen aren't responsible enough to live off-campus.

_____

_____

_____

_____

_____

_____

_____

_____

_____

_____

_____

_____

_____

Answer: *III* should be changed to a subpoint of *II,* since it is one supposed reason why freshmen need supervision.

Acceptable _____   Unacceptable _____

A speaker leaves gaps in his main points when he fails to include all the major ideas. Although this error is less common than overlapping, it does happen occasionally, as the following example illustrates.

Exercise 4.8:

Overlook the other errors, and try to find the gaps in this outline.

Brief History of Transportation

    I.   Man, for thousands of years, walked from one point to another.

    II.   As he developed mentally, his capacity for understanding the living creatures around him increased, and he used animals to transport his goods.

   III. The wheel, history's most outstanding proof of the intelligent supremacy of man, contributed to rapid growth and expansion.

   IV. The wheel has led us to all other forms of land or air transportation: cars, trains, airplanes.

Answer: This outline overlooks water transportation entirely, as well as such categories of air and land travel as ballooning, gliding, sleding, skiing, and skating.

Acceptable _____   Unacceptable _____

This outline contains two other serious errors which violate the rules discussed in this chapter. Can you identify them?

Answer: *II* and *III* each contain two ideas—one related to man's intelligence, the other to transportation. *III* and *IV* overlap.

Acceptable _____   Unacceptable _____

     5. **Whenever possible, main points should have parallel structure.**
These points have parallel structure:

I.   Freshmen need the social life offered by a dorm.

II.   Freshmen need the supervision offered by dorm parents and counselors.

The best use of parallel structure is in revising lists of reasons, characteristics, or
steps.

Exercise 4.9:

*Write the following outline as complete, parallel main points. Use complete
sentences. The first sentence has been done to help you get started.*

"Steps in Studying"

  I.   Preliminary survey

 II.   Read for understanding

III.   Test yourself

IV. Taking notes

 V.   Reviewing

VI. If necessary, reread.

 I. Conduct a preliminary survey of the chapter.

II. _____

_____

_____

_____

_____

_____

_____

_____

_____

Comparison Answer:
  I. Conduct a preliminary survey of the chapter.
 II. Read the chapter for understanding.
III. Test yourself on the contents.
IV. Take notes by underlining.
 V. Review your notes.
VI. If necessary, reread the material.

Acceptable _____   Unacceptable _____

Parallel structure can make the speaker's organization more understandable and memorable, and can add emphasis to his ideas. One student used parallel structure effectively to dramatize the possibility that some food additives have harmful effects. The main points were:

I.   Research has shown a definite link between undesirable side effects in laboratory animals and the use of cyclamates as artifical sweeteners.
II. Research has shown a definite link between monosodium glutamate and "Chinese Restaurant Syndrome."
III. Research has shown a definite link between DES (dielhylstelbestrol) and cancer in mice.

The wording of the points—*"Research has shown a definite link . . ."*—served as a reinforcer for the seriousness of the problem and helped the audience remember the speaker's ideas.

The speaker in the following example would have benefited by the use of parallel structure to clarify and emphasize thoughts and to carry home the central idea that physical education is a necessary part of the school curriculum.

Exercice 4.10:

Can you do a better job of making the main points parallel?

I.   Through physical education comes the development of physical fitness.
II. Physical education leads to the development of social and emotional skills.
III. Participation in physical activities enhances the development of specific motor skills.

Place your revised, parallel main points here:

_____

_____

_____

_____

_____

_____

Comparison Answer:
I. Physical education develops physical fitness.
II. Physical education develops social and emotional skills.
III. Physical education aids the development of specific motor skills.

Acceptable _____   Unacceptable _____

As you have seen, there are a number of valuable uses for parallel structure. An additional one is that parallel structure can help you check the equivalency of your points. Difficulty in making one main point parallel with three others may suggest that the point is actually a subordinate idea.

However, there are also situation in which parallel structure for main points is meaningless or impossible. For example, in a speech on child beating, if the first main point is that child beating is a serious problem, and the second one is that new legislation is needed to cope with the problem, there is little to be gained by saying:

I.   Child beating is a serious problem.
II. Child beating can be helped by new legislation.

Parallel structure is a refinement added to your main points. While refinements are desirable, identifying main points is more important than wording them. Frequently, placing main points in parallel form can be saved for the "Wording of the Speech" step, discussed in Chapter 10. Perhaps the best statement of the rule is "use parallel structure if possible, but don't waste time on it during the organization stage."

Summary of Rules for Main Points

Main points are the supports or reasons for accepting or believing the central idea, so each main point must be directly related to the central idea. There are five rules for writing main points:

1. Each main point should be a complete sentence.
2. Each should contain only one idea.
3. All main points should be of equal importance.
4. They should not overlap or leave gaps.
5. Wherever practical, they should have parallel structure.

SUBPOINTS AND SUPPORTING MATERIAL

In addition to a central idea and main points, a well-organized speech usually has subpoints and supporting material. Subpoints are like main points in that they are statements which must be proved or explained by supporting material. In general, the rules for writing main points apply to subpoints; so, no special rules or practice are give here.

Supporting material is the "evidence" of the speech—the definitions, examples, facts, and descriptions which elaborate or substantiate the subpoints and main points. This traditional model of a speech is depicted in Figure 1 and in the diabetes outline.

A frequent variation of this model is the speech which consists of main points and supporting materials, but no subpoints. Usually this speech is one to inspire or to entertain. It is made up almost entirely of examples, anecdotes, and quotations which have been selected for their relationship to a few major conclusions the speaker wishes to present.

Although a speech without subpoints is acceptable, a speech without supporting material is not. Such a speech becomes a series of generalizations, and without proof or explicit explanation, the audience fails to accept or understand the speaker's proposition. Typically, a speaker presents a speech without supporting material for one of two reasons: he is unprepared, or he failed to limit his subject adequately before he began. The outline on page 56 consists entirely of main points and subpoints and is very well organized. However, it is much too broad for the seven-minute period allotted to the speaker. If supporting material were added for each point, there would be enough material for several hour-long lectures. *In preparing your speeches, be sure to limit the number of main- and subpoints so that you have time to include supporting material.*

OUTLINE COVERING TOO MANY TOPICS*

Specific purpose: to inform the audience of the steps I feel we must take to avoid population-ecological disaster.

   I. We must act immediately to bring our population under control.
      A. A system of financial rewards and penalties needs to be legislated.
          1. We need to reverse our income tax encouragement of reproduction.
          2. We need to reward voluntary sterilization.
          3. We need to make adoption procedures simple.
          4. We need to put a luxury tax on baby items.
      B. Sex education must be mandatory in *all* schools.
          1. The "birds-and-the-bees" approach should be eliminated.
          2. Sex should be shown *not* as a reproductive function.
      C. Population-related research must be expanded.
          1. Effective contraceptive methods should be found.
          2. Human sex determination should be researched.
  II. We must act immediately to eliminate deleterious effects on our environment.
      A. Industrial-automotive air pollution must be eliminated.
      B. Pesticide pollution of air and elsewhere must be eliminated.
      C. Industrial-sewage pollution of waterways must be eliminated.
 III. We must create an atmosphere in which the necessary changes, investigations, and planning can take place.
      A. We must change from a growth-oriented, exploitative system to one focused on stability and conservation.
      B. We must correct our social nearsightedness.

SUMMARY

You will be using the rules covered in Part One as you study the remaining chapters; so, if you're uncertain about them, take time for a quick review now. In Part Two, you will be creating your own outlines complete with central ideas, main points, and subpoints.

---

*This outline covers too much material for one speech. Several topics should be eliminated.

part two

structuring ideas

Part One was a review of the skills which you must have before you begin organizing your speech. These skills include the ability to construct correct outlines, to write correct central ideas, and to prepare good main points and subpoints.

In Part Two, you will begin the study of how to organize. In Chapter 1 we introduced the concept that organization is the process of giving structure and sequence to thought. The chapters in Part Two cover creating the structure; the chapters in Part Three are concerned with sequencing the elements of the speech in logical patterns.

The speech structure of main points, subpoints, and supporting material is shown in Figure 1 on p. 28. These elements combine to form content units which support the central idea, as shown in Figure 2. The speech structure indicates what material will be included in the speech and identifies the relationships among the various parts.

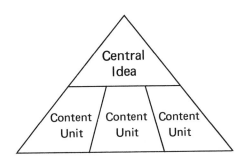

Figure 2.   Content units support the central idea.

However, the speech structure does not predict the sequence in which these ideas will be presented. Because we're used to reading from left to right, we assume that the point on the extreme left of Figure 1 will be given first, but the structure does not dictate this arrangement. The question of order of presentation is part of the sequence step.

Your job as a speaker is to create a structure of central idea, main points, subpoints, and supporting material for each speech that you give. As Chapter 3 explained, before you can create a structure, you must select and narrow the subject, and identify the general and specific purposes. In short, you have to complete the planning stages of speech preparation before moving on to the building stage.*

Part Two, Chapter 5, is concerned with the creative process of structuring a speech. The chapter begins with a discussion of one approach to building a speech structure: analyzing the topic. Analysis of the topic is essentially a planning approach, in which the speaker identifies a tentative central idea and main points (and sometimes subpoints) before conducting his research.

The second half of Chapter 5 is concerned with some guides to analysis of the topic. These guides are standard types of divisions used to break down a central idea into main points or a main point into subpoints. Use of the standard types of divisions speeds the planning stage and helps to create a speech structure that will be clear to the audience.

Chapter 6 takes a more formal look at speech structure. The rules for division identify some of the most frequent errors that speakers make in structuring their ideas.

Chapter 7, "Classification of Material," examines the process of creating structure, as does Chapter 5, but under a different set of conditions. Chapter 7 approaches speech structuring with the assumption that, for any of a number of reasons, the speaker has not completed the planning stages before gathering material. Instead, he starts with supporting material and sets out to create a structured speech. Thus, he is starting at the bottom of the pyramid and is working upward.

Whether the speaker begins at the top of the structure with analysis of the topic or at the bottom with classification of materials, the end result is the same: the creation of a speech structure. The rules for division covered in Chapter 6 will apply equally to the structure, whether it is begun from the top or the bottom.

---

*The stages of speech preparation are discussed in Chapter 1.

5

Analysis of the Topic

INTRODUCTION AND OBJECTIVES

This chapter continues the discussion of speech structure begun in the Introduction to Part Two. The emphasis in Chapter 5 is on the kinds of activities involved in creating your own central ideas and main points for speeches. The chapter offers a number of guides, including analysis charts and standard types of division, to make the job of creating a speech structure easier.

After completing this chapter, you should be able to:

1. Create an analysis chart which limits the topic.
2. Identify a central idea through analysis.
3. Identify main points and subpoints through analysis.
4. List the standard types of division.
5. Create main points and subpoints by using each of the types of division.
6. Select the type of division appropriate to a central idea and specific purpose.

BEGINNING WITH DIVIDING

One way to visualize the need for analysis of the topic is to imagine yourself faced with large birthday cake which you are going to serve to several friends. If you were to begin by cutting a triangular piece out of the middle, your friends would wonder what you were doing. If you then proceed to dig out a square in another section of the cake, your friends would probably take the knife away, because we expect cakes to be divided in some recognizable, uniform pattern— not with haphazard cuts.

Dividing things uniformly, whether they are cakes or speech topics, requires some advance planning. If you want to serve a cake, you must decide where to begin cutting it. If you have to choose a speech topic, you must select a central idea and then decide how to divide the central idea into main points and subpoints to create your speech structure.

This planning is called analysis of the topic. Analysis is an important factor at four stages in the development of a speech: 1) in limiting the subject; 2) in determining the central idea; 3) in finding the appropriate basis of division from which to prepare main points; and 4) in discovering the supporting points which reinforce the main points.

Limiting the Subject
and Determining the Central Idea

Most of us begin preparing a speech by selecting a broad subject we're interested in, such as football, education, pollution, or cancer. These kinds of topics are so general that they cannot be managed in a single speech. In fact, they have been referred to as "warehouses of subjects," because innumerable speeches may be created about any of them. Thus, the first need is to divide the subject into parts and to select one part for your speech.

One effective way to see how much of a warehouse your topic is and to break it down is to draw a chart like Figure 3, which analyzes student housing. The chart represents a series of decisions. The speaker decided to divide student housing on the basis of off-campus and on-campus housing. Since he knew more about on-campus housing and since most of the audience lived on-campus, he continued analyzing on-campus and ignored off-campus. Although both dorms and apartments were available on-campus, the speech was limited to dorms and dorm life, since he lived in a dorm.

On line 5, he listed topics related to dorm life by identifying social life, facilities, and rules as important aspects of dorm living. He considered two possible specific topics for the speech, one under facilities and another under rules, before deciding on "what equipment you need to live comfortably in a dorm." Thus, he used analysis of the topic, combined with other considerations for choosing and narrowing a subject,* to narrow the subject down to the stage of stating a central idea. Since the specific topic was not a complete sentence, he revised it into this central idea: "You need several special items in order to live comfortably in a dorm."

---

*Refer to other sources for information on selecting and choosing a subject.

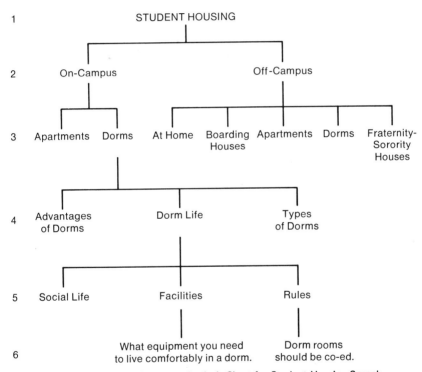

1   STUDENT HOUSING

2   On-Campus   Off-Campus

3   Apartments   Dorms   At Home   Boarding   Apartments   Dorms   Fraternity-
                                    Houses   Sorority
                                                            Houses

4   Advantages   Dorm Life   Types
   of Dorms   of Dorms

5   Social Life   Facilities   Rules

6   What equipment you need   Dorm rooms
             to live comfortably in a dorm.   should be co-ed.

Figure 3.   Speech Structure Analysis Chart for Student Housing Speech.

Exercise 5.1:

Now analyze the topic of dating (male-female social interaction). Break it down to a central idea by drawing a chart like Figure 3.

Write at least one central idea (from your chart) according to the rules in Chapter 3.

Central Idea: _____

_____

_____

Comparison Answer: There is no correct or incorrect answer on the chart, as long as it's a breakdown of the topic. You may compare your chart with the comparison chart in Figure 4 to see how someone else limited dating to a central idea. Then check your central idea to make sure it follows the rules.

Acceptable _____   Unacceptable _____

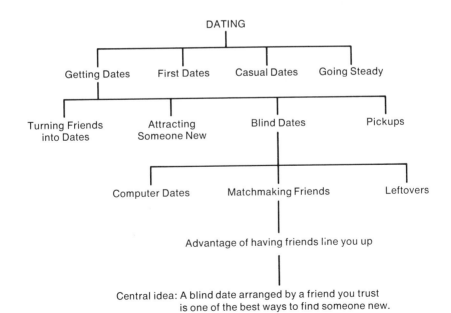

Figure 4.   Analysis Chart of "Dating."

An analysis chart isn't needed for every speech you give. It is most helpful when you have a general topic but are having difficulty focusing on a specific area. Whether or not you use a chart to identify the central idea, you should *identify your central idea before gathering material for the speech.* As the discussion in Chapter 3 indicates, the central idea acts as a guide in deciding what to look for and in eliminating irrelevant material while you are looking, reducing your total preparation time.

Identifying Main Points and Subpoints

So far we have discussed analysis of the topic as an aid in limiting the subject and in determining the central idea, but analysis also applies to finding the divisions for main points and subpoints. A chart can easily be extended beyond the central idea to show the main points and subpoints, since the fundamental thought process is the same: identifying the related subcategories which support the idea being divided. For example, the speaker on student housing (see Figure 3) broke down his central idea into these main areas:

Several Special Items Needed
to Live Comfortably in a Dorm

Food for Snacks   Cooking Equipment   Items for Recreation

Figure 5.   Analysis Chart Identifying Main Points

Once he had identified the main ideas through analysis, all he had to do to create finished main points was to apply the rules for writing main points discussed on page 45.

Exercise 5.2:

Write the divisions on the central idea on dorm living (Figure 5) as complete main points. If you need to refer to the rules, they're on page 45. The first main point has been done as an example.

Central Idea: You need several special items in order to live comfortably in a dorm.

I. You need your favorite foods to supplement what you get in the cafeteria.

Comparison Answer:
II. You need a couple of handy cooking appliances.
III. You need some items for recreation.

Acceptable _____   Unacceptable _____

In the last example, the main areas were identified for you. However, when writing speeches, you will have to identify your own points. So, in the next exercise, you will be given a central idea and asked to think of some reasons to support it.

Exercise 5.3:

Identify some main points for the following central idea on dating.

Central Idea: A blind date arranged by a friend you trust is one of the best ways to find someone new, because:

(Main points)

I.   It's less risky than dating a stranger none of your friends know.

II. _____

_____

_____

III. _____

_____

_____

IV. _____

_____

_____

Comparison Answer: Your answers don't have to be the same as these. You may have mentioned some of the following points:
II. Your friend knows what you like.
III. You're guaranteed at least one evening out.
IV. It's hard to meet new people on your own.

Acceptable _____ Unacceptable _____

The same process is used to divide a main point into subpoints. You are identifying the reasons which will support or explain that main point. In the dating example, if your main point were that "your friend knows what you like," you could explain what you meant by adding subpoints such as "he knows your personality and interests" and "he knows what you like in the opposite sex." Then, of course, you would elaborate on each of these subpoints by adding supporting material.

Exercise 5.4:

What are some possible subpoints for this main point from the last outline?

III. It's hard to meet people on your own.
  A. You keep seeing the same old faces and never someone new.

  B. _____

_____

_____

Comparison Answer: Possibilities are:
B. The male-female ratio around here is unbelievable.
C. Everybody's going steady.
D. Girls and guys travel in separate groups; so it's hard to meet the other sex.
(And the sad tale could be much longer.)

Acceptable _____ Unacceptable _____

Using Analysis of the Topic

Analysis of the topic works well when the speaker is familiar with the subject, because he can identify in advance what the central idea and main points will be. For example, I can decide, as quickly as I can write the words, that I will speak on why students should use this book. My main points will be that it contains realistic examples, provides practice, and spells out clearly the steps students must follow in organizing their speeches. To finish the speech, I will have to come up with subpoints and supporting material for each of these main points, but that can be done rapidly if I use the central idea and main points as guides.

Analysis of the topic also works well when the speaker is unfamiliar with the topic but knows enough to be able to define what he wishes to say and what he needs to learn. Even if the speaker doesn't know the details of a former president's life, he may decide in advance that he wishes to limit his speech to what the ex-president has done since he left the White House. (This approach will work only if the speaker knows history well enough to pick a president who didn't leave in a coffin.) Using analysis of the topic to identify the central idea and main points will make gathering material easier, since the speaker will know exactly what to look for.

TYPES OF DIVISION

The standard types of division aid the speaker in analyzing topics with which he is not particularly familiar, because the groupings suggest some widely used ways that subjects can be broken down into subordinate ideas. Division, as it is used here, has a specialized meaning. *It is the way that a heading is broken down into subheadings.* For example, you may divide a heading *chronologically*—on the basis of time periods. If the central idea is how the time of day affects your mood, the main points might deal with how you feel in the morning, the afternoon, and the evening. These main points are a chronological division of the central idea, and a chronological breakdown is one of the standard types of division.

Traditionally, there are five standard ways to divide a heading: chronological, spatial, cause-effect, problem-solution, and topical. These approaches may be used to divide a central idea into main points and to break down main points or subpoints.

As you will learn in Chapter 9, a strong relationship exists between the type of division and the sequence in which ideas are presented. If you master the ideas presented in this chapter, you will find Chapter 7 and 9 much easier.

Chronological

Many speeches, particularly informative ones, depend heavily on chronological or sequential development. Biographies, accounts of historical events, instructions on how to do something—all are typically developed by main points which identify major steps or periods. Three of the most common types of chronological divisions are ones based on: *time periods* (e.g., 16th, 17th, and 18th century American fashions); the *past, present, and future* (e.g., the development of mass transportation); and *steps in making or doing X* (e.g., how to grow an organic garden).

Exercise 5.5:

Divide the following topic into main points.

Central Idea: There is something good about every season of the year.

I. _____

_____

II. _____

_____

III. _____

_____

IV. _____

_____

Comparison Answer. This exercise is an example of divisions based on time periods. Your points will differ, but they should cover the four seasons:
  I. *Spring* is sunny and green.
  II. *Summer* is vacation time.
  III. *Fall* is crisply beautiful.
  IV. *Winter* is time to relax.

Acceptable _____   Unacceptable _____

Divide this central idea according to past, present, and future.

Central Idea: Today's methods of communication differ from the ones used in the past and the ones likely in the future.

I.   In the past, _____ —

_____

_____

_____

_____

_____

_____

_____

_____

_____

Comparison Answer:
   I. In the past, messages were delivered by hand.
  II. Today, we have electronic equipment to aid communication.
 III. Future scientific inventions may drastically change how man communicates.

Acceptable _____   Unacceptable _____

Many organizations use a special form of the past-present-future division for oral reports on company projects. Such reports, often given on a regular basis to keep management informed of project activities, usually summarize the accomplishments of the last period, describe the activities currently underway, and outline the plans for the next few months.

One of the most common uses of chronological development is to subdivide the first main point to provide some background on the situation. However, as the following exercise illustrates, the use of sequential development may come under any point.

Exercise 5.6:

Provide the subpoints under main point II.

Specific purpose: to show how to make a peanut-butter-and-jelly sandwich.

  I. Equipment needed
 II. How to make it

    A. _____

    _____

    _____

    _____

    _____

    _____

    _____

    _____

    _____

    _____

Comparison Answer: Everyone has his own favorite way of making this kind of sandwich. Mine is:
A. Spread one piece of bread with peanut butter.
B. Spread jelly on top of peanut butter.
C. Eat as an open-faced sandwich.

Acceptable _____   Unacceptable _____

Although chronological division is easy, it is often misused by speakers who practice the word *chronological* and forget that *division* requires some major groupings of ideas. As a result, we get the speaker who gives listeners a year-by-year account of the life led by a famous statesman, when he could limit the report to the statesman's contributions as a lawyer, a legislator, and an ambassador. *Chronologically divided speeches involve more than a listing of items; they must still have two to five major divisions which are meaningful to the audience.*

Exercise 5.7:

Below is a description of a speaking situation which you may face some day. As you read the description, try to determine what serious mistake you made in preparing your speech.

Student government financed your trip to a three-day conference on student athletics, requesting that on your return you give the student council a report of your trip. When you give the report, you begin by describing your departure, where you stayed, and what you did during the first night. You explain that registration and two speakers were on the agenda for the first morning, followed by a luncheon. You continue in this fashion, giving a complete chronological report of how you spent the three days.

What was your mistake? _____

_____

_____

_____

_____

_____

_____

_____

Answer: You failed to realize that they didn't want a minute-by-minute account of how you spent your time; they wanted to know what you had learned. You should have described the major happenings of the conference which concerned your school. Of course, you probably wouldn't have made the mistake if they had been more specific about what they wanted to learn from your report.

Acceptable _____   Unacceptable _____

Spatial

Spatial or geographical division is done on the basis of physical location. The United States is divided into regions; the earth is divided into continents; a building is divided into floors.

Exercise 5.8:

A speech on American food was divided spatially according to regions of the country. You don't have to cover the whole country, but try to provide at least two main points. The first one is started to help you.

Central Idea: Each region of the U.S. has distinctive foods.

I. New England is known for _____

_____

_____

_____

_____

_____

_____

_____

_____

_____

_____

Comparison Answer: Some possible points are:
  I: You're in New England when the soup of the day is always clam chowder.
  II. You know you're in the South if the menu offers grits.
  III. You've hit the Southwest when Mexican food appears on the menu of even the smallest cafe.
(My apologies for not including the great food specialties of the rest of the regions.)

Acceptable _____   Unacceptable _____

     Spatial division has the same potential for misuse as chronological division. If the breakdown begins at too low a level, the speech becomes a long, dull list. Can you imagine listening to a speech in which someone describes the principal industries in each one of the fifty states, rather than grouping them by region? This example is extreme, but the same problem occurs in speeches like one on baseball. If each player is treated as a main point, the speech has at least nine main points, rather than the recommended two to five. The problem can usually be solved by creating more general points and *making subpoints of the items in the long list.* For example, the baseball outline may be handled like this:

I.   Six players are positioned within or near the infield.
    A. The catcher . . .
    B. The pitcher . . .
       (and so on)
II. Three players are positioned well back in the outfield.
    A. The right fielder . . .
    B. The center fielder . . .
    C. The left fielder . . .

Cause-Effect

Cause-effect speeches are concerned with problems. A speaker's purpose may be to inform the audience that the problem exists, to convince them that the problem is a serious one, or to persuade them that the problem is caused by a factor which they hadn't considered before. But the cause-effect speech does not propose a solution for the problem; that is the goal of the problem-solution speech, which will be discussed next.

In dealing with problems, the speaker has three choices: he may talk about the effects of the problem, about the causes, or about both. A student could have as his specific purpose to inform the audience that alcoholism is a serious problem by talking about the effects of alcoholism: broken homes, traffic accidents, absenteeism from work, expense of legal and medical treatment, and so on. He could talk about how to identify a potential alcoholic, with the emphasis on recognizing the causes of alcoholism as they happen. Or he could give an informative speech about the relationship between traffic accidents and alcoholism, first showing that there is a serious problem (the effects), and then explaining how alcoholism increases the traffic accident rate (the cause). Thus, there are several possible cause-effect divisions.

To use a cause-effect division, decide which one of the alternatives you're going to use—are you going to focus on the causes of the problem, the effects, or the relationship between the causes and effects? Then, through thinking and research, identify the specific causes and/or effects that you wish to discuss.

Exercise 5.9:

Divide this central idea into effects and causes. The main points are effects, and the subpoints are causes. To help you, part of the outline has been filled in.

Central Idea: Pets are lots of trouble.

I.   They are _____, because:

    A. _____

        _____

    B. _____

        _____

    C. _____

        _____

II. They are _____, because:

    A. _____

        _____

    B. _____

        _____

    C. _____

        _____

Comparison Answer: (If you're an animal lover, be tolerant!)
I. They are expensive, because:
    A. You have to buy food.
    B. You have to pay for cages or shelter of some sort.
    C. You have to pay for medical care.
II. They are time-consuming, because:
    A. They must be fed and cleansed.
    B. They need affection.
    C. They need exercise.

Acceptable _____   Unacceptable _____

Frequently, when a speaker is giving a persuasive speech, he will describe his proposed change and then will discuss some benefits which will result from the change. This approach is an application of cause-effect division. The change is the cause, and the benefits are the expected results.

Exercise 5.10:

You may disagree with the idea, but identify a number of possible beneficial effects which would result from the change.

Central Idea: We'd all be better off if girls shaved their heads.

_____

_____

_____

_____

_____

_____

_____

_____

_____

Comparison Answer:
   I. Girls would get ready for dates faster.
   II. They would buy more hats and wigs, so employment in these businesses would increase.
   III. It would be much easier to spot girls.

Acceptable _____   Unacceptable _____

Problem-Solution

The problem-solution speech is generally more complex than any other type of speech, as it typically uses cause-effect division in discussing the problem and topical division in discussing the solution(s). In its most elaborate form, a problem-solution speech has the following parts:

I. There is a serious problem which needs fixing.
    A. Background
    B. Effects
    C. Causes
II. There are a number of possible solutions.
    A. Solution X is . . .
    B. Solution Y is . . .
    C. Solution Z is . . .
III. X is the best solution.
    A. It solves the problem.
    B. It is desirable.
    C. It is practical.

Although the problem-solution speech is complex, the speaker usually has no trouble identifying main points, because there are a number of standard areas of concern. Most problems, such as pollution, juvenile delinquency, and drugs, have a history; so they can be discussed in terms of their *past, present,* and *future.* We recognize that a problem exists because we feel its unpleasant *effects;* we know that it came into existence because of certain *causes.* There are several *possible solutions* to the problem, each with advantages and disadvantages in such areas as *workability, practicality, cost,* and *desirability.* These standard areas are usually the main points and subpoints for a problem-solution speech.

Problem-solution speeches are generally persuasive in nature, since the speaker wishes to convince the audience that the proposed solution is the best one. Occasionally an informative speech can be built around solutions to a problem, if the speaker discusses impartially the advantages and disadvantages of several solutions, but informative problem-solution speeches are rare.

Exercise 5.11:

Use a problem-solution division to create a speech on the subject of litter. Identify the problem as your first main point, some possible solutions as your second point, and the best solution as your final main point. Some guides are written in the left margin to help you complete the outline.

Central Idea: Our school should do something about the litter problem.

Problem   I. _____
(Undersirable
effects)   _____

                 A. _____

                 B. _____

                 C. _____

Possible
solutions

II. _____

_____

A. _____

B. _____

C. _____

Best
solution

III. _____

_____

A. _____

B. _____

C. _____

Comparison Answer:
Outline on Litter Problem

I. The litter problem is worse than ever.
  A. The lawn is covered with trash.
  B. The mess around the food machines is unbelievable.
  C. Litter is even bad within the classroom.
II. There are a number of things we can do to cut down on litter.
  A. Provide more waste baskets.
  B. Close the food machines.
  C. Start a publicity campaign on antilittering.
  D. Fine litterbugs.
  E. Sentence litterbugs to a half hour of trash gathering.
III. The best solution is a combination of *A* and *C* in *II.*
  A. It should relieve the problem because
    1. More wastebaskets should prevent littering.
    2. The publicity campaign should encourage picking up trash.
  B. It is more desirable than *B, D,* or *E.*

Acceptable _____   Unacceptable _____

Topical

Topical division is used most frequently since it covers the ways of treating a subject that are excluded by the four types just discussed (chronological, spatial, cause-effect, and problem-solution). You are dividing a subject topically if you approach it on the basis of:

1. *Functions, activities, or parts of a system, institution, or mechanism.* (The State Department of Education has three primary functions; The essential parts of an engine are . . .)
2. *Reasons.* (There are at least four reasons why honesty is the best policy for college students.)
3. *Characteristics, qualities.* (Top-grade beef has these characteristics: . . .)
4. *Organizations or groups.* (The three major civil rights organizations are . . .)
5. *Kinds, types, or categories.* (There are several kinds of life insurance: . . .)
6. *Similarities and differences.* (Comparing two things, such as the educational systems of the U.S. and the U.S.S.R.)
7. *Advantages and disadvantages.* (Pros and cons of changing from quarters to semesters)
8. *Definition.* (Nonverbal communication is . . .)

This list isn't meant to be all-inclusive, but it should provide some examples of the most common topical divisions.

Often, a topically divided speech involves several of the eight categories listed above. For example, a speech on astrology might begin with a definition of astrology, explain how astrologers make their predictions, and discuss the reasons people believe in astrology.

Exercise 5.12:

Write topical main points for the following central ideas.

Central Idea: There are many advantages to living in a small town.

_____

_____

_____

_____

_____

_____

_____

Comparison Answer:
   I. People are friendly.
  II. It's safer in a small town.
 III. The scenery is great.
 IV. The life style is slower and more relaxed.
  V. It's less expensive because there's no place to spend your money.

Acceptable _____   Unacceptable _____

Central Idea: Newspapers serve a number of important functions.

_____

_____

_____

_____

_____

_____

_____

Comparison Answer:
   I. They keep you informed of what's happening in the world.
  II. They publicize local events.
 III. They provide entertainment.
 IV. They're a guide to sales and services.

Acceptable _____   Unacceptable _____

SUMMARY

This section has been a brief overview of the process of analyzing a topic. Essentially, analysis means that the speaker plans in advance what the structure of central idea, main points, and subpoints will be, and then uses the structure as a guide in selecting supporting material.

Analysis works well in situations where the speaker is familiar with his material. In other cases, he may have to do research and classification of material before he can identify his structure. As the examples demonstrated, analysis demands a series of decisions, since there are a number of possible divisions for any one heading. In deciding how to divide his topic, the speaker is guided by his interests and by those of the audience, as well as by an understanding of the effect that he wishes to achieve.

In addition, he should consider the characteristics of each of the five standard types of divisions: chronological, spatial, cause-effect, problem-solution, and topical. *Most speeches will use several types of division—one for the main points and others for the subpoints under each main point.* Remember that the divisions are part of the speech structure and can be created either by analysis of the topic or by classification of material.

6

Guides for the Division Process

INTRODUCTION AND OBJECTIVES

In Chapter 5, the emphasis was on the creative aspect of structuring a speech, and the examples were designed to help you think of main points and sub-points. This chapter provides some checks on the process of speech structuring, in the form of eight rules for division. The eight rules are based on the kinds of errors students make most frequently in organizing their speeches. The exercises are designed to help you identify the errors, suggest ways to eliminate them, and provide practice in revising outlines.

After you finish Chapter 6, you should be able to:

1. Identify divisions which violate the rules.
2. Suggest alternative ways to remove the violations.
3. Revise outlines to remove the violations.
4. Create divisions which do not violate the rules.

RULES FOR DIVISION

As defined in Chapter 5, *division is the way that a heading is broken down into subheadings.* Chapter 5 dealt with how to create divisions through analysis and contained the five standard types of division used in most speeches. This chapter identifies the common errors which students make in structuring their speeches and offers eight rules designed to help avoid these mistakes. The eight rules are guides for good speech structure. You'll probably notice some similarity between the rules for division and the rules for writing main points discussed in Chapter 4, since the divisions are sets of main points and subpoints.

1. **Divide so that all subheadings* are related to the superordinate idea.**† This may seem obvious, but many audiences have been confused by differences between what the speaker said he would say and what he actually said. For example, one student identified as the central idea, "Let us look at how we can prevent and cure those persons afflicted with mental deficiencies." However, the main points were that "research has made the environmental causes clearly evident" and that "science is continually probing into the role of heredity in causing mental deficiency." Clearly, these two main points did not cover the topic that was announced. Instead, the real central idea was buried in the introduction: "The primary causes of mental deficiencies are heredity and environment." This speaker committed the error of creating main points which did not directly support the stated central idea.

Such errors may arise during the initial analysis, when the speaker fails to isolate a clear central idea or prepares tentative main points which include a tangent or two. Just as often, the problem arises after the research stage, when the material that the speaker was able to find creates changes in the content of the speech, but these changes are not reflected in the central idea.

In order to avoid these problems in your own speeches, you should *compare main points with the central idea, and subpoints with main points, at every stage of development* to make sure that they cover the same territory. When subheadings are not related to the superordinate idea, there are three things you can do to solve the problem:

Do more research. Obviously, this solution will work only if the problem is a main point or subpoint which lacks supporting material. The advantage of doing more research is that if you can find the needed material, you won't have to alter the structure of your speech. However, extreme difficulty in finding material for a point may mean that the point is not related to the rest of the speech and should be excluded.

Revise, eliminate, or add main points. There may be a way to revise one of the main points so that it is compatible with the central idea, the other main points, and the supporting material. If you have no supporting material for a point, or if it is less essential to the central idea, you may decide to eliminate it. Sometimes you will discover that your original thought process left gaps or that you have collected some very interesting information which wasn't anticipated in your tentative structure of central idea and main points; so you will add another point. *If you make any changes in the main points— through revision, elimination, or addition—you must make the necessary changes in the central idea.*

---

*Subheadings may be main points or subpoints.
†The use of superordinate and subordinate terms is explained in Chapter 3.

Revise the central idea. This approach may seem the easiest one, but it should be used cautiously. The central idea is more than just a sentence written at the top of an outline. If you refer back to the discussion on page 35, you will realize that a change in the central idea may alter the specific purpose of the speech and may demand changes in the main points, subpoints, and supporting material. Since, theoretically, you choose the central idea carefully before you begin research, be careful in making subsequent changes.

Time is an important factor in deciding between the three alternatives. Since you may not have time to do the additional research needed to fill out the area outlined in the original central idea, you may revise or eliminate a main point and change the central idea. Or you may have the material but lack the speaking time to present all of it, so that again you are forced to revise the main points and central idea.

Exercise 6.1:

The following example is from a speech to entertain. Which main point is not related to the central idea? What would you do to fix the outline?

Central Idea: Crucial information on cheerleaders' knowledge of sports.

    I.   Must know when the team scores.
   II.   Must know when referee is unfair.
  III. Must know latest cheers.
  IV. Must know right words to use in cheers.

_____

_____

_____

_____

_____

_____

_____

_____

Answer: *III* is not related to the central idea. The easiest way to fix the outline would be to drop *III* completely.

Acceptable _____   Unacceptable_____

Now rewrite the central idea so that it is a complete sentence.

_____ _____

_____

_____

> **Comparison Answer:** A successful cheerleader has to know certain things about sports.
>
> Acceptable _____ Unacceptable _____

Exercise 6.2

What's the problem with this central idea and main points? What would you do to fix them?

Central Idea: Chewing tobacco is better than smoking it.

   I. Advantages of chewing over smoking
      A. Keeps your hands free
      B. No lung pollution
  II. Kinds of chewing tobacco
 III. What to do with the juice

_____

_____

_____

_____

_____

_____

> **Answer:** *II* and *III* aren't related to the central idea. Either develop the points under *I* more fully, making them the main points, or revise the central idea so that it covers all three points.
>
> Acceptable _____ Unacceptable _____

Revise the central idea so that it reflects the main points.

_____

_____

_____

_____

_____

_____

_____

_____

_____

_____

_____

_____

Comparison Answer: You should know the advantages of chewing tobacco, the kinds, and what to do with the juice.

Acceptable _____   Unacceptable _____

2. **Divide all coordinate points according to the same system.** This instruction simply means that you should decide who or what you're talking about and then stick to it. Don't try to categorize the material according to several different systems. For example, if you start describing a baseball field as it looks from home plate, finish in that way—don't switch to what you see from left field. If you're listing the benefits of newspapers for the reader, don't throw in how much they help businessmen, as the following example does:

Central Idea: There are several benefits to reading a newspaper daily.

  I.   The reader knows what's happening in the world.
  II. The reader learns about entertainment opportunities.
III. Businessmen who advertise in newspapers get more customers.

In this example, the third main point is not consistent with the approach identified in the central idea.

Exercise 6.3:

This outline suffers from mixed approaches. Can you identify them?

I. Crime is caused by
    A. Poor police protection
    B. Poor living conditions
    C. Unemployment

_____

_____

_____

_____

Answer: *B* and *C* are possible contributing factors which might *cause* someone to commit a crime, whereas *A* refers to inability to *prevent* or deter crime. Thus, *A* is in a different category. Perhaps the speaker needs another main point on deterring crime.

Acceptable _____   Unacceptable _____

Exercise 6.4:

One speaker used three approaches in discussing shoplifting. Try to identify the three from the following selected portions of the outline.

Specific Purpose: to inform the audience on detecting a shoplifter and the consequences if caught.

I. Phases of detecting a shoplifter
    A. Methods of detection
        1. Look for clothes with places to conceal merchandise.
        2. Look for swivel head and roving eye.
    B. Method of surveillance
        1. Don't watch eyes.
        2. Work close in crowded stores.
    C. Apprehension
    D. Interview and decision

II. How to handle special cases of shoplifters
   A. Those who claim illness
   B. Pregnant shoplifters
   C. Elderly shoplifters
III. Punishment of shoplifters
   A. Petit larceny may mean six months in jail or $300 fine.
   B. Grand larceny may mean imprisonment for up to five years.
IV. How to prevent shoplifting
   A. Two-way radios
   B. Cameras
   C. Security guards

Can you identify the three conflicting approaches?

_____

_____

_____

_____

_____

_____

_____

_____

_____

_____

Answer: Points *I* and *II* are from the point of view of the person handling the shoplifter; point *III* deals with the individual shoplifter; and point *IV* talks about what the store can do. (Note: The specific purpose used in this example is one which should be revised, as should the whole outline.)

Acceptable _____   Unacceptable _____

3. **Divide so that points are coordinate and are subordinate to the same concept.** The main points of a speech should be equal in importance and should provide support for the central idea of the speech. If you're not sure about the terms *coordinate* and *subordinate* or about the relationship of the central idea and main points, review the discussion on pages 28-35.

Exercise 6.5:

Identify the main point which is not coordinate with the others.

   I.   America has become an apathetic society.
  II.   Examples of people's lack of caring for others.
 III. What can we do to reduce apathy?

The main point which is not coordinate is _____ .

Answer: *II*

Acceptable _____   Unacceptable _____

Revise the outline to remove the error in main point coordination. While you're at it, remove the other errors in outline construction.

_____

_____

_____

_____

_____

_____

_____

_____

_____

_____

_____

_____

_____

_____

_____

Comparison Answer:

I. America has become an apathetic society.
   A. People don't care for others
      1. Example
      2. Example
II. There are several things we can do to reduce apathy.
(Make sure that in your revision *II* is not a question.)

Acceptable _____   Unacceptable _____

---

4. **Divide so that the different units do not overlap.** Overlapping is actually an error in coordination because the overlapping usually occurs when a subpoint is listed as a separate main point.

Exercise 6.6:

In the following outline can you identify which two points overlap and which one is actually subordinate to the other?

Central Idea: Cigarette smoking is not only harmful to your health but also brings on many more problems.

   I. Cost
      A. For the cigarettes themselves
      B. Expense of damages caused by cigarettes
  II. Inconveniences
      A. Time consumed
      B. Mental anguish when unable to smoke
      C. Inconvenience to those who are allergic to smoke
 III. Filthy
      A. Ashes everywhere
      B. Smoke pollution
  IV. Health
      A. Cancer
      B. Contributes to heart disease

The two points which overlap are _____ *and* _____ . *The subordinate point*

is _____ .

Answer: The overlapping points are *II* and *III*. Filthiness is one inconvenience caused by smoking; so, *III* is subordinate to *II*.

Acceptable _____ Unacceptable _____

Revise the outline to eliminate the overlapping and put III where it should be. For extra practice, write each main point as a complete sentence, using parallel sentence structure.

_____

_____

_____

_____

_____

_____

_____

_____

_____

_____

_____

_____

_____

_____

_____

_____

_____

_____

_____

Comparison Answer: (for outline on cigarette smoking)
I.   Cigarette smoking is expensive.
    A.   Smokers spend a large amount yearly for cigarettes.
    B.   In addition, they must pay for damages caused by cigarettes.
II. Cigarette smoking creates inconveniences for smokers and nonsmokers.
    A.   Smokers waste time purchasing and smoking cigarettes.
    B.   "No-smoking" situations cause problems for the smoker.
    C.   Smoking is annoying and often physically irritating to nonsmokers.
    D.   Smoking is filthy.
    E.   Smoking contributes to air pollution.
III. Cigarette smoking endangers your health.
    A.   It is heavily connected with lung cancer.
    B.   It is a main contributor to heart disease.

Acceptable _____   Unacceptable _____

5. **Divide so that the representative parts or elements of the field are covered.** The subpoints should provide a comprehensive development of the point being divided. The shoplifting outline, for example, neglected such areas as describing the problem of shoplifting or discussing who shoplifts and why. An example of an outline which omits some of the representative elements is the following one on "A Brief History of Transportation."

I.   For thousands of years man walked from one point to another.
II. As he developed mentally, his capacity for understanding the living creatures around him increased, and he used animals to transport his goods.
III. The wheel, history's most outstanding proof of the intelligent supremacy of man, contributed to rapid growth and expansion.
IV. The wheel has led us to all other forms of land or air transportation: cars, trains, airplanes.

Exercise 6.7:

What areas has the speaker omitted? (If you read this example in Chapter 4, the answer should be easy.)

_____

_____

_____

_____

_____

_____

_____

_____

_____

_____

_____

_____

_____

_____

_____

_____

Answer: The speaker has overlooked water transportation entirely. In addition, he has omitted such forms of land and air transportation as balloons, gliders, sleds, skiis, and skates.

Acceptable _____   Unacceptable _____

6. **Divide so that one subdivision does not equal the whole subject.** As we indicated in Chapter 4, true one-point speeches are rare. Sometimes a speaker gives the appearance of having a one-point speech because he hasn't identified all his points or he keeps repeating the same idea in each "new" point. These are errors in analysis which the speaker should avoid.

Exercise 6.8:

What is the problem with this outline?

Specific purpose: to tell why exercise is beneficial to the body

I. Telling how exercise is good for the body
II. Taking the heart as a muscle and explaining the effects of exercise on the heart as a muscle and why there is a need for exercise

The problem is: _____

_____

_____

_____

_____

_____

_____

_____

Answer: *I* says the same thing as the specific purpose, and *II* is a repetition of *I.* This outline doesn't have any real divisions.

Acceptable _____   Unacceptable _____

7. **Usually, divide to have at least two and no more than five main headings or parts.** When there are more than five main points, the audience has a difficult time remembering them all. Besides, the amount of time allotted for most speeches isn't enough to develop numerous main points adequately. Sometimes the number of subheadings will exceed five, as in the case of the nine symptoms in the diabetes outline but, whenever possible, try to limit the number of divisions.

One way to reduce the number of headings is to group ideas together and combine them under one superordinate heading. A speaker had nine pieces of advice on "how to make worrying constructive." Rather than listing all nine as main points, they were collected into three larger groups.

Exercise 6.9:

Nine pieces of advice are listed as subpoints in the outline below, but the main points are left out. Try filling in the main points, and see how close you come to the original main points.

I. _____

    _____

    A. Don't worry about situations which can't be changed.
    B. Don't worry about problems which *you* can't solve.
    C. Don't worry about things which aren't likely to happen.

II. _____

    _____

    A. Correct and study mistakes instead of worrying about them.
    B. Turn errors into assets.
    C. Remember that mistakes are a necessary part of the learning process.

III. _____

    _____

    A. Instead of avoiding worrisome situations, think of them as challenges.
    B. Analyze the situation completely.
    C. Balance worries with blessings.

Comparison Answer:
  I.   Worry realistically.
  II. Learn from worries.
  III. Take a positive approach to problems.
(Your answers will differ from the points listed here, but you should now have a better understanding of how to avoid using long lists of points.)

Acceptable _____   Unacceptable _____

    8. **Create your own divisions—don't try to follow the arrangement of a single source.** Some of the worst mistakes in organization come from trying to use material in exactly the same way some magazine article or newspaper story did. Most teachers require students to use more than one source so that they will avoid this error, but some students still try to use only one source, or

they try to use one source for 95 percent of the speech and the dictionary for the rest. The problem with this practice is that your audience and specific purpose probably will differ from the author's, and there are differences between oral and written presentation, so that what was a clear *written* message may be confusing to a listener.

In addition, the article may contain more material than you can present in the allotted time, or the material may be irrelevant to your central idea. *It is up to you to include only the relevant material, and to organize it in a way that will support the central idea and specific purpose.*

The following outline is an example of what happens when a student tries to present material from one source in its entirety, rather than formulating a central idea and then selecting only material which relates to this idea.

Exercise 6.10:

This outline is based on a magazine article. The questions after the outline should help you to identify the errors and suggest ways of remedying them.

Central Idea: To inform the class on statistics about rape, the disbelief its victims are subjected to, and unfair laws which make conviction for this offense almost impossible in some states.

  I. Statistics on rape
 II. Reasons for lack of reporting assault by victims
III. Reasons for mistrust of victims by law officers and courts and humiliation inflicted by them
    A. Once a victim goes to the police, the chain of events is difficult to stop.
    B. First step is hospital exam.
    C. Many hospitals refuse to examine rape victims.
    D. Police station is next and often ugly experience.
       1. Victims say police seem to get pleasure out of hearing details of crime.
       2. Victims say they think police believe they are lying.
       3. Police say they judge truth by reported amount of resistance.
       4. Police often ask personal questions about victim's sex life which don't relate to the crime.
       5. Following police arrest of assailant, victim must tell story to a district attorney, to a grand jury, testify at preliminary hearings, and then at trial in open court. This procedure may last for two years.
       6. Some people believe that a woman cannot be raped by one man or that she really wants to be raped. Others believe that she deserves what she gets, as if she must have seduced the assailant.
       7. In some states, pregnancy caused by rape does not fall under the category of cases which qualify for legal abortions.

Now answer the following questions about this outline:

1. Did the central idea agree with the main points as to the content of the speech? Why or why not?

_____

_____

_____

_____

_____

_____

_____

> **Answer:** *No,* because there was not a main point related to unfair laws, although this material was included, and because the second main point is not identified in the central idea.

Acceptable _____   Unacceptable _____

2. Is this central idea a good one? Why or why not?

_____

_____

_____

_____

_____

_____

_____

> **Answer:** *No,* because it is not a clear, simple statement of what the speech is to cover. It shows that the speaker has tried to include everything in the article, rather than choosing a central idea and then selecting only material pertinent to this idea.

Acceptable _____   Unacceptable _____

3. Do the main points cover approximately equal amounts of material? (Circle one)

   YES   **NO**

   Which main points aren't developed? _____

   Answer: *NO* should be circled, as *I* and *II* aren't developed with supporting material.

   Acceptable _____   Unacceptable _____

4. *III* is divided by several different approaches, rather than just one. List the conflicting approaches. (Remember Rule 2.)

   _____

   _____

   _____

   _____

   Answer: There are at least five approaches: steps victims go through, problems that victims have, attitudes of police, general beliefs about rape, and laws related to rape. Such a mixture is not an effective way to present material.

   Acceptable _____   Unacceptable _____

5. Can you identify the errors in coordination in points *A-D* under *III*? Identify the problem.

   Problem: _____

   _____

   _____

   Answer: *A* is superordinate to *B* and *D; C* is subordinate to *B*.

   Acceptable _____   Unacceptable _____

Revise points A-D to eliminate the problem. _____

_____

_____

_____

_____

_____

_____

_____

_____

_____

_____

_____

_____

_____

Answer:
A. Once a victim goes to the police, the chain . . .
   1. First step is hospital exam
      a. Many hospitals refuse . . .
   2. Police station is next . . .

Acceptable _____   Unacceptable _____

6. Does *A* (as revised in the last answer) support *III*? What should be done with *A* and its subordinates?

_____

_____

_____

Answer: *A* does not support *III*, and probably should be a main point.

Acceptable _____   Unacceptable _____

7. There are errors in coordination in the seven points under *D*. How many of the seven are really subordinate to *D*?

_____

_____

_____

Answer: The first four.

Acceptable _____   Unacceptable _____

8. What points are coordinate with *5*? What should be done with *5*?

_____

_____

_____

Answer: *5* is coordinate with *B* and *D*, since it's the third step in the process. It should be made a coordinate point related to the judicial process, with the specifics listed as subordinates under it.

Acceptable _____   Unacceptable _____

9. What should be done with *6-7*?

_____

_____

_____

Answer: The best alternative may be to eliminate them entirely. Failing that, they should become a new main point, since they are not related to the rest of the material under *III*.

Acceptable _____   Unacceptable _____

USING THE RULES FOR DIVISION

The rules for division are designed to help you produce better main points and subpoints. As a quick review, the rules are:

1. Divide so that all subheadings are related to the superordinate idea.
2. Divide all coordinate points according to the same system.
3. Divide so that points are coordinate and are subordinate to the same concept.
4. Divide so that the different units do not overlap.
5. Divide so that the representative parts or elements of the field are covered.
6. Divide so that one subdivision does not equal the whole subject.
7. Usually, divide to have at least two and no more than five main headings or parts.
8. Create your own divisions—don't try to follow the arrangement of a single source.

Once you have followed the eight rules and produced the ideas which will be your main points and/or subpoints, you can continue with the process of preparing your speech, by:

1. Stating each idea clearly in complete sentences, using parallel construction where appropriate.
2. Making any necessary subdivisions.
3. Assigning supporting material to each point.
4. Checking over the points and supporting material for appropriateness to the audience and to your specific purpose.

SUMMARY

The structure of a speech is defined by the content units. Deciding what ideas will be in each content unit is a creative challenge for the speaker. The types of divisions (Chapter 5) will help the speaker invent tentative main points and subpoints, while the rules for division will help evaluate the points and place them in the total structure of the speech.

7

Classification
of Material

INTRODUCTION AND OBJECTIVES

The ability to classify related material under appropriate headings, creating the
headings if necessary, is an important skill for the speaker. Classification of
material is used in preparing every speech, since supporting material must be
assigned to fill out the speech structure. The use of classification often extends
beyond matching up material with the part of the structure that it supports;
classification is frequently used to help create the total structure.

As Chapter 5 stressed, whenever possible the speaker should identify
the tentative central idea and main points before gathering supporting material.
However, for a number of reasons—among them lack of knowledge about the
subject or a request for a speech based on supplied materials—the speaker will
not always be able to conduct this preliminary planning. Then he must begin
with the supporting material and create his speech structure by grouping related
ideas and abstracting headings for the groups.

After completing this chapter, you should be able to:

1. Assign subordinate material (either subpoints or supporting
   material) to the point it supports.
2. Identify main points and subpoints.
3. Create headings which cover a group of subordinate ideas.
4. Identify material which can be eliminated from a speech to
   adapt to the audience, purpose, or other requirements of the
   speaking situation.

BEGINNING WITH THE MATERIAL

Classification is the process of grouping like things together and giving the new group a name. Thus, classification depends heavily on the ability to recognize subordinate and coordinate relationships and on the ability to create or abstract superordinates for groups of coordinate items. As a process, classification must be done after the material-gathering stage, whether the material is obtained through library research or from the speaker's personal experiences.

Classification is used both to identify structure and to assign supporting materials. Basically, the process involves grouping related ideas together to form the bottom levels of the outline or speech. Sometimes the main points and subpoints will be included in the material or will have been identified previously by analysis; at other times you'll have to create points to cover subgroups of ideas.

One advantage of using classification to create the structure is that the points actually relate to the material. However, the chances of errors in coordination and division are greatly increased; therefore, *outlines produced by classification should be checked closely against the rules for division.*

Ideally, classification should be combined with analysis of the topic, so that the structure identified by analysis is a tentative outline, subject to modifications during and after the research stage. Whenever possible, the speaker should conduct a preliminary analysis of the topic, identify a tentative structure of main points (and perhaps of subpoints), use the structure to guide his research, and compare the material obtained through research with the needs of the tentative outline.

If he discovers that he has just the material called for, he is ready to go on to the next stage of speech preparation. If there are discrepancies between the tentative outline and the researched information, he must do more research, change the central idea, and/or change the main points (either by addition, elimination, or modification). This combination of analysis and classification is generally the most effective way to produce speeches with clear organization.

However, there are situations in which other approaches are called for. Sometimes a speaker is handed a mass of information and is told to produce a speech from the information; so, he must rely entirely on classification to produce the complete structure of main points, subpoints, and supporting material.

Occasionally, the brainstorming approach is useful, either for preparing a speech or for writing a theme on a subject which requires no research. The "brainstorm-and-classify" approach involves listing, as rapidly as possible, everything you can think of related to the central idea or topic. This list includes generalizations, examples, quotations, solutions, and so on. Later on you may decide that much of the list is irrelevant, but initially the goal is to create a long list quickly. Once the list is complete, follow the typical classification approach: grouping related ideas together, eliminating unnecessary material, identifying superordinate ideas, and, if necessary, creating superodinates.

PRACTICE IN CLASSIFYING AND ABSTRACTING

This chapter is designed to give you practice in performing the skills involved in using classification to assign material to points and to create points which cover subgroups of ideas.

Assigning Points to Headings

The following exercises in classification are designed to help you gain skills so that you can use classification effectively in preparing your own speeches.

The first series of exercises requires you to identify coordinate ideas and place them under the appropriate superordinate ideas. You use this skill to create a basic outline of main points and then assign the supporting material to the appropriate points.

Exercise 7.1:

The three main points are identified. A list of seven subpoints follows the skeleton outline. From the list, find the supoints which support each main point.

Central Idea: Advertising campaigns can be divided into three major stages.

I. The planning stage

    A. _____

    B. _____

II. The execution stage

    A. _____

    B. _____

    C. _____

III. The evaluation stage

    A. _____

    B. _____

Place the number of the subpoint in the blank under the main point that it supports.

1. Coordinating advertising with other promotional methods
2. Analyzing results against objectives
3. Determining objectives and goals
4. Creating message or copy
5. Obtaining results of the campaign
6. Analyzing the marketing situation
7. Scheduling media

Answer: Under *I* should be *3* and *6; 1, 4,* and *7* support *II;* and *2* and *5* are subpoints under *III*.

Acceptable_____   Unacceptable_____

Exercise 7.2:

In the last exercise, the main points were identified for you. In this exercise, you will have to identify the main points in the list and then assign the subpoints.

Central Idea: Wise planning in four areas can save money on medical bills.

1. Local community hospitals are less expensive for common illnesses.
2. You should keep your insurance up-to-date.
3. Ask your doctor to prescribe drugs by generic names.
4. Having one regular doctor is the cheapest form of medical care.
5. Investigate the costs and services of hospital care.
6. Investigate group insurance policies, since they give more benefits per dollar spent.
7. Large medical centers and university hospitals are more expensive.
8. Choose a family doctor and visit him regularly.
9. Use a discount-store pharmacy if possible.
10. Be sure that your insurance policy contains all benefits that you may need.
11. Periodic checkups catch illness early and eliminate the costs of major illnesses.
12. Make a comparative drug-price check.

What are the four main points? Identify them by number in the blank.

_____

Answer: The main points are *2, 5, 8,* and *12.*

Acceptable _____   Unacceptable _____

Which subpoints support 2? _____

Answer: *6* and *10* are the subpoints under *2,* since they are concerned with insurance policies.

Acceptable _____   Unacceptable _____

Which subpoints would you assign to 5? _____

Answer: *1* and *7,* which discuss hospitals.

Acceptable _____   Unacceptable _____

By now there are only four subpoints left. Which two support 8, and which go with 12?

_____

_____

_____

_____

Answer: *4* and *11* support *8; 3* and *9* support *12.*

Acceptable _____   Unacceptable _____

Exercise 7.3:

The exercise that you just finished was fairly simple once you identified the main points. The next outline is more complex, because some of the subpoints are subdivided into a second level of supoints; that is, the outline will have three levels:

I. _____

    A. _____

        1. _____

However, not all of the A-level subpoints are divided; so, you'll have to be on your toes.

Specific Purpose: to inform the audience that child beating is a problem, why parents do it, and what is being done about it.

1. Present laws have too many loopholes.
2. Some steps are being taken to prevent child beating.
3. Sense of self-righteousness.
4. Children can be passed off as victims of accidents.
5. People hesitate to report suspected child beating.
6. Stricter laws have been passed.
7. Child battering is uncontrolled.
8. The laws don't provide enough punishment.
9. Organizations are being formed to help parents.
10. Children interfere with parents' relationships.
11. It is difficult to diagnose cases of child battering.
12. Parents beat their children for many reasons.
13. States are setting up centers to help in diagnosing battered children.
14. Laws are not strict or modern.
15. Psychotic parents.
16. General physicians aren't skilled at diagnosing child beating.

What are the three main points? (Refer back to the specific purpose if you have trouble deciding.) Identify the main points by number in the blank below.

Answer: The main points are *2, 7,* and *12.*

Acceptable _____   Unacceptable _____

Which items on the list are related to 7, which would be the first main point presented in the speech?

_____

_____

_____

Answer: *1, 4, 5, 8, 11, 14,* and *16* all help to establish that child beating is a problem.

Acceptable _____   Unacceptable _____

Which items are subpoints for 12, which would be the second main point presented?

_____

_____

_____

Answer: *3, 10,* and *15.*

Acceptable_____   Unacceptable _____

As if you couldn't guess, which items are subpoints for 2?

_____

_____

_____

Answer: *6, 9,* and *13.* (Isn't it nice to get an answer right?)

Acceptable _____   Unacceptable _____

Now construct an outline for the first main point, using subpoints 1, 4, 5, 8, 11, 14, and 16. Do not rewrite the sentences. Instead, put the number of the sentence beside the symbol.

I.   7 _____

   A. _____

     _____

     _____

     _____

     _____

     _____

     _____

     _____

     _____

     _____

Comparison Answer:

I.   (7) Child battering is uncontrolled.
   A.   (11) It is difficult to diagnose cases of child battering.
      1.   (4) Children can be passed off as victims of accidents.
      2.   (16) General physicians aren't skilled at diagnosing child beating.
   B.   (5) People hesitate to report suspected child beating.
   C.   (14) Laws are not strict or modern.
      1.   (1) Present laws have too many loopholes.
      2.   (8) The laws don't provide enough punishment.

Your answer may list the subpoints in a different order, as long as you used the correct symbols and assigned the subpoints to the right point.

Acceptable _____   Unacceptable _____

Creating Headings

This set of exercises relates to the ability to create headings which cover a group of related points. In other words, given the coordinate ideas, you are to create appropriate superordinate points.

Exercise 7.4:

Provide main points for the following subpoints.

Central Idea: There are differences between the registered nurse (RN), the licensed practical nurse (LPN), and the nurse's aide.

I. _____

_____

_____

_____

    A. The RN is required to have the highest degree of training.
    B. The LPN has one year of training.
    C. The nurse's aide has six months of training.

II. _____

_____

_____

_____

    A. The RN directs and supervises.
    B. The LPN assists coworkers.
    C. Certain procedures and duties are performed by the nurse's aide.

Comparison Answer:
  I. Each kind of nurse requires different amounts and kinds of training.
 II. Each type of nurse has specific duties and responsibilities.

Acceptable _____   Unacceptable _____

Exercise 7.5:

Below are four details related to unidentified flying objects (UFO's). Come up with a point (more general idea) that this information would support.

A. _____

_____

1. The first reported flying saucer was seen on June 24, 1947, near Washington's Mount Ranier.
2. On January 7, 1948, three UFO's were spotted on Air Force radar.
3. On July 24, 1948, two Air Force pilots spotted a wingless craft about 100 feet long.
4. In April, 1959, a UFO collided with an Air Force C-118 near Sumner, Washington.

Comparison Answer: Since 1947, there have been many reported encounters with UFO's.

Acceptable _____   Unacceptable _____

Classifying Ideas

We said earlier that one approach to speech construction is to brainstorm and list all the related ideas, and then go back and group them.

Exercise 7.6:

Here are the ideas one student listed as essential steps in job hunting. Read the steps, and then try to group the steps into three major stages. Write your suggested stages in the blanks below the steps.

1. Read the want ads.
2. Arrange for recommendations.
3. Go to employment agencies.
4. Visit places where you'd like to work.
5. Learn about the company before the interview.
6. Be on time for the interview.
7. Appearance counts—be neat and clean.
8. Call or write for an appointment.
9. Be polite but direct in asking for an interview.
10. Fill out forms carefully.

Major Steps:

I. _____

II. _____

III. _____

Comparison Answer: Your answers should be similar to:
Finding job openings
Applying for an interview
Preparing for an interview

Acceptable _____   Unacceptable _____

Now, using the suggested answers as main points, complete the outline by writing in the number of the step under the correct stage.

I. Finding job openings

_____

_____

_____

II. Applying for an interview

_____

_____

_____

III. Preparing for an interview

_____

_____

_____

_____

Answer: Under *I* should be *1, 3,* and *4;* under *II, 8, 9,* and *10;* and under *III, 2, 5, 6,* and *7.*

Acceptable _____   Unacceptable _____

Exercise 7.7:

A student was assigned to give an informative speech, and he chose as his topic "Mosquitoes." Since he didn't know anything about the topic, he was unable to perform a preliminary analysis of it. The following is the information that he collected during his research stage. As you read his material, try to group it into five or six categories.

1. Over 2,500 varieties
2. Of the order Diptera
3. Gnats and flies are also Diptera.
4. Only female bites
5. Female makes noise
6. Mosquitoes attracted by brunettes over blondes
7.   ″   ″   ″ dry skin rather than wet
8.   ″   ″   ″ dark clothing over light
9.   ″   ″   ″ activity
10.   ″   ″   ″ warm skin
11.   ″   ″   ″ stinky nonbather rather than clean person
12. Mosquitoes bite twelve times an hour.
13. Mosquitoes weigh four times as much after drinking blood.
14. Need animal's blood at least once so that eggs can develop
15. Males eat fruit and plant juices.
16. Mosquito eggs are usually laid in water.
17. Eggs pass through four larval stages.
18. Complete life cycle may take only one to two weeks.
19. Mosquitoes are found far north of the Arctic Circle.
20. They carry such diseases as malaria, yellow fever, and human encephalitis.
21. Natural enemies of adults are dragonflies, damselflies.
22. Fish eat larva.
23. There are problems with use of insecticides, and swamp drainage threatens balance of nature.
24. One method of mosquito control is spreading oily substance on infested water.
25. Less chance of being bitten if you stand still
26.   ″   ″   ″   ″   ″   ″ ″ wear light clothing
27.   ″   ″   ″   ″   ″   ″ ″ take cold showers every ten minutes or so
28. Also less chance if you don't breathe
29. Mosquitoes like CO_2 (carbon dioxide).
30. Orlando, Florida, man put in room with three dummies. He was safe as long as the air he exhaled was drawn off. When it wasn't, 300 mosquitoes attacked.

Identify five or six categories which may be used to classify this information.

_____

_____

_____

_____

_____

_____

Comparison Answer:
General information
Information about mosquito bites
What attracts mosquitoes
Life cycle of the mosquito
Mosquito control (natural and man-made)
Avoiding mosquito bites

Acceptable _____   Unacceptable _____

Assume that you are to give a five-to-seven minute informative speech on mosquitoes. Your central idea is: "Knowledge about the mosquito and why it bites may save you some itching this summer." *What categories of information (in the last answer), if any, would you eliminate in preparing your speech?*

_____

_____

_____

_____

_____

_____

Answer: Because of the time limitation, eliminate information on the life cycle and mosquito control, which are less directly related to the central idea.

Acceptable _____   Unacceptable _____

If you were presenting a 5-minute report on the mosquito in biology class, which categories would you eliminate?

_____

_____

_____

Answer: The categories related to what attracts mosquitoes and how to avoid bites, since they're probably not what the instructor wants you to present.

Acceptable _____   Unacceptable _____

SUMMARY

Classification of material is more than just saying that "these two things belong together." It is also the ability to identify why the two belong together and to create a name for the new group which was formed by joining two formerly separate items.

part three

sequencing ideas

As you saw in Part Two, one of the speaker's major tasks in organizing is identifying the structure of the speech. Once the structure is complete, he then decides on the sequence of presentation for the main points, the subpoints, and the supporting material.

The two chapters in Part Three deal with how to order material effectively. Chapter 8 is concerned with principles of arrangement which can increase the effectiveness of the speech. The principles in Chapter 8 should help the speaker see how his choice of organization can affect the audience. Chapter 9 covers the five basic orders, which represent standard ways to sequence ideas. It gives the speaker practice in arranging ideas in a variety of patterns.

sequencing ideas

8

Principles
of Arrangement

In completing the exercises in Part Two, you may have noticed that some points seemed to have a built-in pattern, like the four seasons of the year, while the sequence of other points was arbitrary, like the beneficial effects of shaved heads for women. Chapter 8 looks at some of the problems speakers face in arranging their ideas and describes some common principles of arrangement that can help the speaker decide on sequence.

After completing this chapter, you should be able to:

1. Evaluate the advantages and disadvantages of using each of the principles of arrangement.
2. Suggest which principle of arrangement would be effective for a given speaking situation.

THE IMPORTANCE OF SEQUENCE

After the structure of the speech has been identified, the speaker should focus his attention on sequencing the material and ideas of the speech. *The purpose of this process is to arrange material in "a natural sequence of thought that will carry the listener progressively point by point to the acceptance or understand-*

ing of the speaker's purpose."* This remark implies that the sequence in which material is presented can do much to advance or to hinder the speaker's cause.

The truth of this is seen every day. The speaker who asks for money for a charity before he has explained why the charity needs money has little chance of success. Similarly, the history teacher who expects his students to know the key events in four Civil War battles can guarantee a lot of F's by skipping around from one battle to the next and then back to the first. In both examples, the speaker has not given enough thought to how to sequence material so that it will be easy for the audience to understand and accept what he says.

In every speech, the speaker faces the problem of sequence several times, because he must decide on sequences for the main points, the sets of sub-points under each main point, and each group of supporting material. Thus, the principles and orders discussed in this chapter and in Chapter 9 apply to all parts of the speech, although organization of main points is emphasized, since they are the most important ideas.

For many of your speeches, suggestions for the appropriate sequence will come from the central idea, the method of division, and the material itself. A central idea of explaining how to make homemade ice cream implies a step-by-step sequence. A speech concerned with how welfare money gets from the federal government to the individual recipient has two logical starting points: the federal government at the top or the recipient at the bottom of the welfare structure. In a speech on how to begin skiing as a hobby, it makes sense to talk about getting the right equipment before recommending ski resorts.

However, not all speeches have such inherent patterns, so sometimes the speaker must make arbitrary decisions about sequence. There is no magic guide to guarantee the appropriateness of a chosen arrangement for a given topic and audience. But there are some principles of arrangement and basic patterns which the speaker can apply. In making a decision about sequence at any level of the structure, the speaker may find that these principles and patterns will suggest an order for otherwise hard-to-arrange material.

APPLYING THE PRINCIPLES OF ARRANGEMENT

The principles of arrangement identify some of the intuitive ways that we order material. For example, if we are delivering a number of messages to someone, we instinctively tell him the most important one first. If we have several pieces of good news, we may save the best for last. If we're teaching someone how to operate a new machine, we may demonstrate the simple procedures one day and let him practice them before going on to the more complex steps. *In each case, the primary consideration is the effect of the sequence on the listener.* We are

*Eugene E. White, *Practical Speech Fundamentals* (New York: The Macmillan Company, 1960), p. 284.

concerned with the best way of presenting the material to the listener so he will be informed, entertained, or persuaded.

This same consideration for the probable effect on the receiver should operate in preparing a public speech. First and foremost, the speaker is concerned with obtaining a desired audience response. And the sequence of ideas will determine in part whether he obtains that response. *Thus, it is during the stage of sequencing that the speaker adapts his organization to suit his audience.*

In the principles which follow, the important thing is not how the material seems to the speaker but how it impresses the audience. For example, a home economist with a strong interest in food and nutrition is asked to speak to the members of an extension club about meal preparation. To her, the most important point is that the week's menu should be nutritionally sound, whereas her audience is most concerned with cost. Since it is the audience which determines what is important and interesting, cost should be the most important point of the speech, unless the home economist wishes to prove to her audience why they should be more concerned about nutrition.

The basic principles of presentation are:

1. Simple-to-complex or familiar-to-unfamiliar arrangement. In this arrangement, you begin with what the audience understands, and then lead gradually to what is new. You may apply this principle to a speech on forms of government by talking first about the democratic forms similar to ours, then about socialist governments, and finally about dictatorships. This sequence is particularly important in explaining complex or unfamiliar ideas to the audience.

Exercise 8.1:

If you were explaining football to some visitors from England, how might you apply this principle?

_____

_____

_____

Answer: Talk about what football has in common with soccer, a sport they're familiar with, before going on to how the games differ.

Acceptable _____   Unacceptable _____

2. Agree-to-disagree arrangement. This principle suggests that you tell the audience things they'll agree with before telling them things with which they're likely to disagree. A teen-ager uses this approach when she asks her father, "Don't you think exercise is important?" as a prelude to asking for the money to take up skiing. Beginning with agreement is a good persuasive strategy, because it makes the speaker seem "like a reasonable guy who understands how we feel," instead of "that idiot who got up there and told us we were crazy."

Exercise 8.2:

Read the description, and then decide how you could apply the principle of agree-to-disagree.

"You believe that the only way that population growth can be controlled effectively is to enact legislation which restricts family size. You are to speak on this subject to a club which is concerned with overpopulation and is actively involved in disseminating information on birth control and sex education. The group has gone on record as opposing mandatory limitations on family size."

What area of agreement could you begin with?

_____

_____

_____

_____

_____

_____

_____

_____

_____

Answer: You both agree that population growth is a problem, so you could begin by a brief reemphasis of the problem. Since you probably agree that sex education and birth control are necessary, you could tell the audience that you are in agreement on these two methods before you go on to show why they cannot solve the problem alone.

Acceptable _____   Unacceptable _____

Why would this approach be more effective than starting out by telling the club members how ineffective their methods are?

Answer: Most of us react with hostility if someone tells us we're all wrong, and we refuse to listen. We're much more likely to listen if told we're on the right track but need to go one step further.

Acceptable _____ Unacceptable _____

3. Mixed order of interest or importance. The mixed order of importance involves placing your second-most-important point first and your most important point last. This sequence is a way to maintain audience attention throughout the speech.

The reasoning for this sequence is that if you go from least interesting to most interesting *(3-2-1)*, your audience may go to sleep before you get to the best. If you begin with the most interesting, the rest of the speech is a disappointment, and there's nothing left to listen for.

According to research, listeners tend to remember the first and last items in a series most accurately, which is an additional reason for using the mixed order. If you save the best for last and pick the next best point to start out with, the ideas which are most important stand the best chance of being remembered.

To use the mixed order of interest or importance, rank your points or examples in order of importance or interest *to the audience.* Then place the most important point last, the second most important point first, and the other(s) in the middle. This technique applies whether you have three, four, or five main points. As long as you have *the most important point last and the next most important point first,* the order of the middle points is less significant and may vary from situation to situation.

Exercise 8.3:

You're going to present the following ideas to your speech class. Read the central idea and main points, and then decide on an effective order.

Every student should participate in at least one school activity, like student government, a club, or a sport, because:

1. Participation looks good on job applications and increases your chances of being hired.
2. In most cases, it improves your social life, helps you make friends of both sexes, and may mean dates.
3. It's a learning experience, both in how to do things and in how to work with people.
4. It provides a break from the study grind, so that you can go back refreshed.
5. It's a partial cure for self-centeredness, forcing you to look at what others are doing and to work for others.

In what order will you give the five reasons? Why did you choose this sequence?

_____

_____

_____

Answer: *2* and *3* are probably the most important reasons. The members of your speech class probably will be more impressed with *2* than with *3;* so, your order could be *3-5-4-1-2.* (Your order for *1, 4,* and *5* could easily be different.)

Acceptable _____   Unacceptable _____

4. Climactic (3-2-1) arrangement. Climactic arrangement begins with the least important or exiting ideas and moves systematically to the most important or exciting. It has the effect of dramatizing or adding importance. Because of the limitations noted in the discussion of the mixed order, the climactic order is generally less effective than other orders as an arrangement for the main points of a speech, unless the main points are a list of effects or reason.

However, climactic order may be very effective for arranging subpoints or supporting ideas. For example, one way of making a problem seem truly serious is to give a number of examples, each one more horrifying than the last. A second way to use climactic order is in presenting the benefits of a proposed new program, beginning with the lesser benefits and moving to the most significant.

Exercise 8.4:

Read the following problem and then decide how you would sequence the benefits.

You are the refreshment chairman for a club. It's up to you to ask people to bring food or contribute money to pay for the club parties. Somehow, certain members always forget to pay and you've been making up the difference out of your own pocket. You are now broke, so you propose that every member pay $1.00 a month to be used for parties and refreshments. In preparing your speech to the club, you decide to tell club members that the change will have these advantages:

1. It will be easier on everyone's budgets. Some of you have contributed three or four dollars at a time. This way the payments are spread out, so it won't hurt your budget.
2. You won't have to spend as much. Right now a few members are coming to the parties free, and you're paying for them.
3. The job of the refreshment chairman would be lots easier.
4. We'll have everything we need, because the party committee can buy supplies before the party. Remember the hamburger fry where the person with the ketchup and mustard didn't come?

If you were to present these four ideas in climactic order, how would you arrange them?

_____

_____

_____

Comparison Answer: Start with *3*, since it's not as important to the other members as it is to you. Then present *1*, because it is an inconvenience everyone shares. Whether you put *2* or *4* last depends on your sense of values (and those of the club members). Some people care more about the money, while others can't stand parties which don't run smoothly. If your club has been plagued with the absence of vital things (like no bowls or spoons on the night you serve ice cream), *4* should definitely be last.

Acceptable _____   Unacceptable _____

5. Deductive or inductive arrangements. *Most speeches are presented* deductively; *that is, the speaker announces his generalizations or conclusions (the superordinate ideas from his outline) and then proves or explains them.* This procedure is particularly effective for transmitting information and for emphasizing certain points.

However, occasionally there are times when the speaker needs to proceed more indirectly. He may want the audience to draw its own conclusions from the evidence; he may fear that the audience is so opposed to his ideas that they will turn him off if he announces his conclusions in advance; or he may simply wish to add a little dramatic effect. In these situations, *he may present his speech* inductively, *by giving the explanations and examples (the supporting material) first, followed eventually by the conclusions.*

The difference in the two orders can be seen in the following example: Deductively, a speaker may tell his audience that "the high school dropout faces all sorts of problems in today's society," list the types of problems, and tell brief stories about dropouts who have experienced each problem. The same material could be presented inductively by a speaker announcing that he wished to tell about the experiences of five teen-agers. After presenting the five stories, he could say, "Now, what do these five teen-agers have in common? They all dropped out of school," and then go on to summarize the kinds of problems that dropouts face.

The most common use of inductive order is in drawing conclusions from specific examples, particularly for speeches to inspire, to entertain, or to persuade. Rarely is the entire speech presented inductively. In the example of the speech on dropouts, the first part of the speech establishing the problem of dropouts might be arranged inductively, but the speaker would switch to deductive order in discussing solutions.

An alternative way of employing inductive order is to avoid stating conclusions until after they have been established. For example, a speaker may present main points deductively but refrain from stating the central idea of the speech until the end. This method is common in persuasive speeches, where the speaker needs to lay the groundwork for his proposal.

As we said earlier, *the primary difference between inductive and deductive order is the sequence in which ideas are presented to the audience, not the construction of the speech.* Thus, the same preparation outline will serve for either order, so that the speaker can check the relationship of ideas. However, if he wishes to present a portion of the speech inductively, he may prepare a separate speaking outline, which shows the ideas in the sequence he wishes to say them.*

---

*See p. 153 for information on preparing speaking notes for inductive presentations.

Exercise 8.5:

Refer back to the situation described under "agree-to-disagree" on page 120. Would you present your central idea deductively or inductively? Why?

Answer: Present your central idea inductively, at the end of the speech, so that the audience isn't hostile throughout your presentation.

Acceptable _____   Unacceptable _____

SUMMARY

Sequencing is a dynamic skill, as the sequence which moves one audience to understand and accept your central idea may be ineffective with a different group of listeners. Selecting the best order requires careful audience analysis and use of the principles of arrangement. The primary arrangements are:

1. Simple-to-complex or familiar-to-unfamiliar
2. Agree-to-disagree
3. Mixed order of interest or importance
4. Climactic (3-2-1)
5. Deductive or inductive

9

Five
Basic Orders

INTRODUCTION AND OBJECTIVES

Chapter 8 discussed general principles of arrangement which are helpful in deciding how to sequence ideas. A second set of guides to aid in deciding on sequencing are the basic patterns or orders. The five basic orders have the same names as the five types of division discussed in Chapter 5: chronological, spatial, cause-effect, problem-solution, and topical. In the finished speech, the type of division and the basic order are closely related. However, while you are preparing the speech, the two approaches represent separate processes. It is possible for a speaker to decide that he will discuss the foods of each region of the country and to identify his main points without deciding on the sequence in which he will present the main points.

   After completing this chapter, you should be able to:

1. Identify each of the orders.
2. Arrange main points and subpoints in each of the orders.
3. Select the appropriate order for your material.

USING THE BASIC ORDERS

Speech textbooks usually list five basic organizational orders or ways to arrange your material: chronological, spatial, cause-effect, problem-solution, and topical. *The first four orders are patterns, because they suggest the way that you will arrange your material.* In a sense, they give you diagrams from which to choose, so that your task is almost like a fill-in-the-blank. For example, the chronological pattern implies that you arrange material according to a time sequence; the problem-solution suggests that you discuss the problem first and then talk about solutions.

The topical order is used for those divisions which do not fit the other patterns. Instead of following a standard diagram, a topical pattern is derived from the material, the speaker's purpose, or the principles of arrangement. Consequently, topical patterns are the hardest ones to employ, although they are the most common. In fact, this chapter is arranged topically, discussing chronological, spatial, cause-effect, problem-solution, and topical orders, in that sequence.

Chronological Order

The chronological or sequential pattern is developed by arranging the main points in a logical sequence. It is usually a past-to-present arrangement, but the pattern may be reversed to add interest or emphasis. For example, you could describe certain facts of education as they now exist and then go back into the past. Some examples of chronological order follow.

Chronological main points, past-present-future

Central Idea: Air transportation is constantly changing.

    I.   In 1903, the Wright brothers made the first controlled and sustained flight in a power-driven airplane.
   II. World War I brought a rapid advance in airplane design.
 III. After World War II, jets were introduced.
 IV. Now systems permit orbital flights.
   V. At some time in the future, interplanetary spacecraft will be perfected.

Sequential main points

Central Idea: Audience analysis is composed of three main steps.

   I.   Studying the composition, interests, and attitudes of the audience before you speak
  II. Studying audience reaction as you speak.
 III. Studying the audience's reaction after the speech through comments, questionnaires, and surveys

The outline on Valentine's Day is a good example of a topical outline which utilizes a variety of patterns.

Exercise 9.1:

Valentine's Day*

Specific Purpose: to make the audience aware of the history of Valentine's Day and some of the beliefs associated with it.

I. History of Valentine's Day
    A. Contrary to popular belief, the practice of Valentine's Day did not originate with a man named Valentine.
        1. It goes back to ancient Rome.
        2. They celebrated Lupercal.
            a. In honor of Juno, goddess of women and marriage, and Pan, the god of nature.
            b. One long fertility rite
            c. For young lovers
            d. Celebrated on Feb. 15
    B. In 496 A.D. Pope Gelasuis tried to give Christian meaning to the pagan festival of Lupercal.
        1. Changed dated to Feb. 14.
        2. Renamed it St. Valentine's Day.
        3. St. Valentine is one of two people:
            a. Priest in Rome under Emperor Claudius II
                1) Beheaded on Feb. 14, 269 A.D., for protecting Christians
                2) Supposedly cured jailor's daughter of blindness
            b. Bishop of Terni, about sixty miles from Rome, at same time
                1) Converted Roman family to Christianity
                2) Beheaded Feb. 14, 269 A.D., also
    C. St. Valentine's Day was celebrated as early as 1446 in England.
        1. It is mentioned by a number of English authors:
            a. Chaucer
            b. John Gower
            c. John Lydgate
        2. Lovers sent each other gifts and notes.
    D. Valentine's Day became popular in the U.S. about the time of the Civil War.
        1. German valentines were fashionable.
    E. Today millions of valentines are mailed each year, but the day is not religiously significant.

*Stevan Northcutt, speech material prepared at Tallahassee Community College (unpublished), 1972.

II. Beliefs associated with Valentine's Day
   A. They center around love, courtship, marriage.
      1. "Birds choose their mates on this day."
   B. Most are for single women looking for husbands.
      1. "It's bad luck to bring snow drops into the house if any single female residents are to be married in the year."
      2. "Look through your keyhole first thing on Feb. 14. If you see two objects, you will marry soon. If you see one, your chances are bad this year."
      3. "Strike your forehead with a rose petal. If it cracks, wedding bells will ring soon."
      4. "Pin five bay leaves to your pillow at bedtime, one in each corner and one in the middle. You will see your future husband in your dreams."
      5. "Write the names of your boyfriends on separate pieces of paper. Roll them into individual clay balls and drop them into a glass of water. The first name to surface will be that of your husband-to-be."

In the outline on Valentine's Day, what pattern is used for the subpoints (A through E) under I?

_____

_____

_____

_____

Answer: Chronological, past to present

Acceptable _____   Unacceptable _____

Spatial Order

Textbooks include spatial order as one of the five basic patterns, although it is rarely used for arranging main points. Its main use is in arranging supporting material under main points. Common spatial arrangements are inside-to-outside, left-to-right, looking-around-the-room-clockwise, background-foreground, or close-to-distant.

The important consideration in using a spatial pattern is to examine each of the parts in a logical sequence, rather than skipping around. For example, if you're talking about interesting cities of the U.S., don't talk about them in this order: San Francisco, New York, Seattle, Chicago, Los Angeles, and Miami—because you force the listener to cross the U.S. five times. A second consideration is identifying a starting point and examining all parts in relation to it.

Exercise 9.2:

Why is this outline an ineffective use of spatial arrangement?

Central Idea: To explain the lay-out of a large city park by looking at a map and working from left to right.

   I.   At your far left is the entrance gate.
  II.   As you enter, straight ahead you will see an amusement area covering approximately ten acres.
III.   To the far right are the docks and picnic tables.
IV.   A train will take visitors back for five miles to the zoo area.
  V.   The farthest point on the map is the camping area and the animal compounds.

Answer: *II* changes to a new starting point—what the visitor sees from the entrance, rather than what the audience sees on the map. *IV* and *V* are not identified in relationship to a starting point, so we don't know where they are.

Acceptable _____   Unacceptable _____

Cause-Effect Order

There are two common causal patterns: cause-effect and effect-cause. In an effect-cause pattern, you might show that certain conditions exist (the effect) and then talk about what caused the problem. In a cause-effect pattern, you might begin with a discussion of certain changes which will be implemented (causes) and describe their anticipated effects. The question of which cause or effect to place first or last is usually answered by one of the principles of arrangement.

Exercise 9.3:

Decide which effects should be presented first and which principle of arrangement to use.

One student was advocating the construction of a large parking lot on campus and listed the following beneficial effects to be derived from the change:

1. More students could use their cars.
2. Visitors would have no problem finding parking spaces.
3. If constructed near the football field and gym, a parking lot would solve the traffic problems at games.
4. Everyone could find a parking space rapidly, so no one would be late to class.

If the audience were the school's alumni association, which effects would you emphasize? In what order would you present the effects?

Answer: Emphasize *2* and *3*. Use the mixed order of importance. Order: *2, 4, 1, 3.* You could begin with *2* to start out with a guaranteed positive effect, end with *3* as a bonus effect if the lot is placed in the right spot.

Acceptable _____   Unacceptable _____

===

Problem-Solution Order

Problem-solution order involves demonstrating that: (1) there is a problem, and (2) the problem can be solved by the suggested solution. Beyond these basics, the speaker has many alternatives, some involving the use of other patterns.

If the audience agrees that the problem exists, the speaker only needs to review it briefly before devoting his major efforts to the solution stage. If, however, he must demonstrate that there is a problem, he can do so by showing that the present system causes undesirable effects. Sometimes establishing the problem will require two steps: 1) showing that a certain situation is desirable and, 2) proving that it is threatened. Thus, in the "Dolphin" outline on page 136, the speaker demonstrates that dolphins are useful to man for a number of reasons but that the dolphin population is in danger of extinction.

The speaker also faces alternatives in his treatment of the solution. He may compare several solutions before urging the audience to accept one. He may simply tell his listeners: "Here are the choices—you decide." Or he may focus on one solution, omitting reference to other alternatives. In any case, he must describe the solution and discuss such aspects as workability, practicality, effectiveness, and desirability, usually in that order.

Topical Order

Topical order is reserved for those headings which have been divided topically. However, as noted earlier, it is misleading to call topical order a pattern, because there is no standard formula for arrangement. Instead, the sequence is suggested by the speaker's purpose, the division of main points, or the principles of arrangement.

An example of the sequence being suggested by the division of main points is a speech about communication in a factory. If the three main points discuss the regular employees, supervisory employees (such as foremen), and management, you would normally begin either with the regular employees and work up, or with management and work down to employees.

Exercise 9.4:

Suppose that you were talking about involvement in local, state, and national politics. What are the two natural sequences for your speech?

_____

_____

_____

_____

_____

_____

_____

_____

_____

_____

_____

_____

_____

_____

Answer: Either local, state, and national; or national, state, and local.

Acceptable _____ Unacceptable _____

Whenever the main points of the speech suggest a natural order, as they did in the examples of factory communication and political involvement, the speaker usually follows them in his speech. The one exception to this rule would be if a change in sequence would adapt the speech to the audience. A speaker talking to a state political committee might fill them in on activities at the local and national levels first, before concentrating on the main order of business, politics in the state.

Exercise 9.5:

How could the sequence be altered to adapt the speech on factory communication to an audience of supervisory employees, such as foremen?

_____

_____

_____

_____

_____

_____

_____

_____

_____

_____

_____

_____

Answer: Discuss the other two levels first, and the supervisory level last, so that the points are arranged climactically in order of interest to the audience.

Acceptable _____   Unacceptable _____

MULTIPLE PATTERNS IN SPEECHES

You may have noticed that although the "Valentine's Day" outline was labeled "topical," other patterns were also used in construction. This mixing is typical of how speeches are developed, with one type of division for main points and others for subpoints and details. For convenience, the order of the main points is used to describe the speech as a whole.

The questions following are designed to help you recognize the different patterns as they are used to create a complete speech.

MODEL PROBLEM-SOLUTION OUTLINE

Saving the Dolphin*

Specific Purpose: to convince the audience that for the welfare of mankind, misuse and killing of dolphins should be stopped.

I. Dolphins are important to man.
   A. It seems likely that dolphins are capable of interspecies communication.
      1. Dolphins have the necessary physical capabilities.
         a. The brain of the dolphin
            (1) Is the same size or larger than man's brain.
            (2) Is advanced enough to communicate systematically.
         b. The dolphin has three communicating apparatuses.
            (1) Two are located in nasal passages or below the blow hole.
               (a) Right side is whistling apparatus.
               (b) Left side is clicking apparatus.
            (2) Third apparatus is located in the vocal chords.
               (a) Emits ultrasonic beam.
               (b) Used for sonar.
      2. Dolphins can make humanized sounds.
         a. This ability was discovered by accident.
            (1) In 1955, Dr. John Lilly was listening to tapes of dolphins.
            (2) They appeared to be mimicking human speech.
            (3) Lilly proved this true by getting a dolphin to copy words.
      3. Dolphins will talk to us through air.
         a. Communication among dolphins is underwater.
         b. Communication with us is through our medium, air.
         c. Dolphins teach others that have had no contact with man to communicate through air to humans and dolphins.
      4. They will answer us in water if we talk to them under water.
   B. Interspecies communication can aid man.
      1. It helps him improve his own communication.
      2. It helps him understand animals of different species.
      3. It could help him in communication with interterrestrial species, that opportunity ever arises.

*Darlene L. Heinrich, speech material prepared at Florida State University (unpublished), 1972.

II. Unless something is done, the bottle-nose dolphin may become extinct along the southern coasts of the U.S.
   A. Tolls are being taken by sewage from cities.
      1. Infection
      2. Illness
      3. Death
   B. Dolphins are being lost by capture.
      1. For entertaining humans in oceanaria around the world
      2. For motion pictures
      3. For television shows
      4. For Navy tasks
      5. For pets
III. To save the dolphin, we should extend the "golden rule" to include dolphins.
   A. The golden rule says, "do unto others as you would like them to do unto you."
   B. Our concept of "others" who are equal to us should include the dolphin, since their brains are as large as ours and they can communicate.
   C. Applying the golden rule to dolphins would solve the problem.
      1. Dolphins would no longer be hunted and captured, since we don't want that to happen to us.
      2. The factors which threaten the dolphins' way of life would be controlled.

Exercise 9.6:

In the outline on dolphins, what function does each main point have?

_____

_____

_____

_____

_____

_____

_____

_____

Answer: *I* and *II* establish the problem by showing that we need dolphins but are in danger of losing them. *III* is the solution.

Acceptable _____   Unacceptable _____

What type of development is used for the subpoints under I?

_____

Answer: Topical.

Acceptable _____   Unacceptable _____

What type of development is used for II?

_____

Answer: Effect-cause.

Acceptable _____   Unacceptable _____

What pattern is used for developing B. The dolphin has three communicating apparatuses?

_____

Answer: Spatial—the location of the communication apparatuses.

Acceptable _____   Unacceptable _____

What kind of development is used for B under I?

_____

Answer: Cause and possible beneficial effects. Inter-species communication is the cause; *1, 2,* and *3* are possible effects.

Acceptable _____   Unacceptable _____

SUMMARY

A well-developed speech will employ a number of types of divisions and patterns. The choice of patterns is influenced by the type of material and the desired effect. The principles of arrangement should be considered in sequencing material. *Remember that the goal of sequencing is to arrange material so that the audience can understand and accept your purpose.*

part four

finishing touches

The previous chapters have discussed what a speaker must do to create an organized speech. Once he has prepared the basic speech, there are several things which can enhance the organization of the speech, thereby increasing its effectiveness. Chapter 10 covers the use of oral organization, the preparation of speaking notes, and the delivery of the finished speech. Chapter 11 sums up the preparation of an organized speech from beginning to end.

10

Delivering an Organized Speech

INTRODUCTION AND OBJECTIVES

Once you have successfully accomplished all of the objectives for the previous chapters, the hard work of speech organization is done. This chapter is concerned primarily with some practical hints which will help your speech sound as good and as organized as possible.

After completing this chapter, you should be able to:

1. Write previews, summaries, and transitions for your speeches.
2. Prepare legible speaking notes.
3. Identify the factors which cause speeches to sound disorganized.
4. Use delivery effectively to enhance the organization of your speech.
   a. Use notes effectively.
   b. Speak fluently.
   c. Avoid telling the audience you are disorganized.
   d. Use oral organization (transitions, previews, and summaries).

THE AUDIENCE'S PERCEPTION OF ORGANIZATION

Let's assume that the speaker now has an organized speech: he has a clearly defined structure of main points, subpoints, and supporting materials, all arranged in appropriate sequences. The speaker still has one more hurdle to conquer before he is through with organization. He must deliver a speech which sounds organized.

Organized in this context has a slightly different meaning; it is concerned with *what makes an audience think that a speech is structured.* This question is important, since organization is related to speaker credibility. Disorganized speakers are considered less credible than speakers rated high in organization, which in turn limits the effectiveness of the speech.

To audiences, organization is equated with announced development, preparation, and fluent delivery. Members of the audience expect the speaker to announce what he will discuss early in the speech, to indicate during the speech when he changes from one major idea to another, and to provide some form of summary at the end. This format (the old "tell them what you're going to tell them, tell them, and tell them that you told them") may seem trite, but it is what an audience expects. *Even when the speech is structured clearly, the audience needs help from the speaker in identifying the plan of development.* To provide this help, the speaker typically uses language devices such as previews, transitions, and summaries.

Preparation and fluent delivery are related, because fluent delivery is seen as a sign that the speaker is prepared. Beyond this assurance, however, the members of an audience expect to see a speaker who uses a minimum of notes, refers to them sparingly, has no difficulty finding what he needs within his notes, makes no apologies, and does no announced backtracking to cover points missed earlier. These and other things the speaker can do to ensure that his audience will recognize his organization will be covered in this chapter.

Preparation

It is a rare speaker who can give an unprepared speech and make it sound organized. Usually this ability is reserved for people who are experts on their subject and have acquired the ability to organize in their heads without preparing a written outline.

For most speakers, being prepared means that the outline is completed enough in advance of the delivery date of the speech that the speaker can: 1) add the introduction, transitions, and conclusion to the outline; 2) practice with the complete outline; 3) prepare a set of speaking notes; and 4) practice delivering the speech from the notes.

The preparation of a speech manuscript will not be discussed in this book, other than to note that the initial preparation stages are the same. However, instead of preparing speaking notes, the speaker writes out the speech word for word.

Wording the Speech

The description of the stages of speech preparation in Chapter 1 indicated that the final stage covered in this text, Wording the Speech, includes two important steps:

1. Polishing main points and subpoints
2. Adding oral organization devices

Polishing main points and subpoints means revising the wording of these points, if necessary, to clarify them and give them parallel structure.

ANNOUNCED DEVELOPMENT: ORAL ORGANIZATION

Readers have a number of visual cues which warn them that the author is moving from one idea to the next. These cues include indentation of paragraphs, numbering of ideas, and headings of different size and location. The listener is less fortunate—he must depend on what the speaker says and does to indicate changes in thought.

Knowing this fact, the good speaker does everything that he can to keep his audience with him. First, he indicates changes through variations in delivery—he modifies his voice, gesture, and position. Second, he announces his changes through the use of certain oral organizational devices: *previews, summaries, and transitions.*

The inclusion of these devices is important, since they tell the audience what the organization of the speech is. Without them the audience may perceive the speech as disorganized, even if it actually has a clear underlying structure. The oral organizational devices have two purposes: first, they specify what the relationship of ideas is (e.g., "these examples show that there is a serious problem. . . ."). Second, they add redundancy to the message; that is, they reiterate the main ideas of the speech, which increases the likelihood that the audience will understand and remember them.

The time to work on oral organization is after the initial outline has been developed, since the preview, summary, and transitions are all based on the main points and subpoints of the speech. While the speech is being developed, oral organization devices should not be included in the outline, as they are generally restatements of the central idea and main points. However, at this stage they should be written in on the copy of the outline that you use for practice. An example of an outline with these sentences added is the outline on diabetes (page 147).

The preparation of each type of oral organization is discussed separately in the following sections.

Previews

A preview gives the members of the audience an idea of what they should be listening for. The most frequent use of previews is as part of the introduction to help the audience focus on the specific areas to be included in the speech. In long speeches, previews also may be used in introducing each main point as the speaker comes to it.

Generally, the preview alone is insufficient to begin the speech; usually it should be preceded by some statements designed to arouse the audience's interest and motivate them to listen. An example of an introduction which includes a preview is:

> Unless you're married or going steady, you probably have the same problem I have—finding people to date. After trying most of the approaches to dating that there are, I've decided that there's only one really effective way to do it: have a friend you trust arrange a blind date for you. I believe in this method for a number of reasons . . .

The need for a preview extends to the speech presented inductively, even if the preview is simply a statement that the speaker wants to present three stories and then draw some conclusions which can be applied to the present situation.

Exercise 10.1:

Write a preview for the Valentine's Day outline on page 129.

_____

_____

_____

Comparison Answer: Since Valentine's Day will be here soon, I thought it would be interesting to talk about the history of Valentine's Day and some beliefs associated with it.

Acceptable _____   Unacceptable _____

The preview need not always be a dry run of what the speaker wishes to say, as long as it tells the audience what the speaker intends to do. For example, a speaker can simply tell his audience that "since litter is a serious problem at our school, I want to talk about some things we should do to solve the problem," without disclosing his solutions until later in the speech. This approach is particularly wise if the speaker anticipates some initial disapproval of his ideas.

MODEL OUTLINE WITH ORAL
ORGANIZATION ADDED

INTRODUCTION: Most of us have heard of the seven warning signals for detection of cancer, but few people know that there are also warning signals for diabetes. Today I want to describe these signals and the types of tests available.

I. Although the actual cause of diabetes is not known, scientists have found certain factors which are related to diabetes.
   A. People over forty (women especially)
   B. Overweight people
   C. People related to diabetics
   D. Women who have shown carbohydrate intolerance during pregnancy
   E. Women who have given birth to large babies (9 lbs.)

TRANSITION: If you can be classified under any of the five factors that I just gave, then it is important that you know the symptoms of diabetes.

II. Knowing the symptoms of diabetes can help you decide if you have the disease.
   A. Symptoms
      1. Frequent urination
      2. Abnormal thirst
      3. Rapid weight loss
      4. Extreme hunger
      5. Drowsiness (may be only symptom)
      6. General weakness
      7. Visual disturbance
      8. Skin infections
      9. Mental disturbance
   B. Example of woman who had some of the symptoms

TRANSITION: If you have any of these symptoms, you may wish to be tested for diabetes.

III. Doctors have several tests by which they can diagnose even mild cases.
   A. Types of tests
      1. Urine test
      2. Blood test
      3. Glucose-tolerance test

  B. Frequency of testing
    1. At least once a year

   CONCLUSION: If any of the factors related to diabetes apply to you, do go to your doctor for testing if any of the symptoms appear.

Exercise 10.2:

For the speech on population control (page 56), would you tell the audience in your preview that your favored solution was mandatory population control? Why or why not?

                       Answer: Don't tell the audience, because you would make them even less willing to listen to you.

         Acceptable _____   Unacceptable _____

Summaries

 A summary is a brief review of what has been covered. The most common form of summary is the list of what was said, although a summary may be a restatement of the idea in other words.

 A summary may be identical to the preview, or it may go into greater detail. For example, the speaker who told his audience in the preview that he would talk about the problem of litter and some possible solutions may say in the summary: "We have seen that we have litter problems in the following areas . . .:" (he would list the problems) "and in order to relieve the problem we must . . ." (he would list the solutions).

Although we most often think of a summary as part of the conclusion of the speech, a speaker also uses internal summaries to review what he has said about one main point before he moves to the next one or to reemphasize a subpoint.

Exercise 10.3:

Write an internal summary of the first main point on page 56 (don't include the subpoints under A, B, and C).

_____

_____

_____

_____

_____

_____

Comparison Answer: In order to bring our population under control, we must do three things immediately: legislate a system of financial rewards and penalties; make sex education mandatory; and expand efforts in population-related research.

Acceptable _____   Unacceptable _____

Transitions

Transitions are connective devices used between phrases, sentences, examples, subpoints, and main points. Transitions may be words, phrases, sentences, or brief paragraphs. They warn the listener that what follows is a totally new idea, or that it is an addition, contradiction, illustration, paraphrase, summary, logical conclusion, or repetition of something just said.

We use transitions naturally in conversation, especially such terms as *and, also, in other words, so, therefore, thus, but, however, then, first,* and so on.

In delivering a speech, the speaker needs to use transitional phrases freely, since they explain the relationship between ideas.

In addition, he should use sentence and paragraph transitions, particularly to signal that he is moving from one point to another. In the speech on diabetes, (page 147), the speaker used effective sentence transitions to move from one main point to the next.

A paragraph transition usually consists of an internal summary of the last main point (one or two sentences) and a preview of the next area. An example of a paragraph transition for the speech on Valentine's Day is:

> "Thus, we see that Valentine's Day has changed gradually through the years from a pagan holiday, to a religious day, to a time for lovers. During this time, interesting beliefs related to Valentine's Day were also being developed. Most of them are concerned with the love aspect of the day, particularly with advice for the young girl seeking a husband."

Paragraph transitions are probably the most important type of transition, since they help the audience to stay with the speaker as he moves from one main area to the next. They also provide emphasis by repeating key ideas. This can be done without sounding monotonous by using synonyms or by referring back to key words. Well-done paragraph transitions are more than a flat statement. "The first main point was that. . . . The second main point is that . . ."

Exercise 10.4:

Write a paragraph transition to be used between the second and third main points in the outline on cigarette smoking (page 91).

_____

_____

_____

_____

_____

_____

_____

_____

_____

_____

_____

_____

_____

_____

_____

_____

_____

_____

Comparison Answer: So far we have discussed two major disadvantages to cigarette smoking: cost, and inconvenience to the smoker and to people around him. There is a third disadvantage which outweighs the others: smoking endangers your health.

Acceptable _____   Unacceptable _____

Using Oral Organization

One rule for using oral organization seems self-evident: *the divisions referred to in the preview, summary, and transitions must be the same as the divisions actually followed in the speech structure.* Unfortunately, some speakers haven't mastered this skill. For example, one student told the audience in the preview that "dreams serve three functions for the psychological well-being of the human mind." However, in the course of delivering the speech, these main points were used:

I. Dreams are hallucinations which occur during sleep.
II. Daydreams are a normal function for escape.
III. Nightmares are the most severe anxiety dreams.

Obviously, these main points represent a different division—according to the types of dreams rather than according to the three functions of dreams. You can imagine the confusion of the audience when the speaker again referred to three functions in the conclusion, as if he had indeed developed them fully in the body of the speech, instead of mentioning them as subpoints.

Exercise 10.5:

The same kind of error occurred in this preview. Make any necessary changes in the preview so that it fits the body of the speech.

Preview: Since everyone at some time has suffered from some form of headache, I think that a little knowledge of the subject would be of value. In presenting some basic information on headaches, first I shall identify some types of headaches; then I shall inform the class about some types of treatment.

I. The characteristics of the migraine headache
   A. The symptoms of a migraine
   B. Some causes of migraines
   C. Possible treatments for migraines
II. The common tension headache
   A. Some symptoms
   B. Causes
   C. Treatment

Put your revision of the second sentence of the preview here:

_____

_____

_____

Comparison Answer:
Preview: I shall discuss the symptoms, causes, and treatment of two common types of headaches: migraine and tension headaches.

Acceptable _____ Unacceptable _____

Now write a transition between the two main points.

_____

_____

_____

Comparison Answer: Although the migraine headache is much more painful than the tension headache, the tension headache is the one which most of us experience from time to time.

Acceptable _____ Unacceptable _____

SPEAKING NOTES

Extemporaneous speaking is used most frequently today, and an important step in the preparation of an extemporaneous speech is the preparation of usable speaking notes. *Good notes are brief, highly readable statements of the high points of the speech.* They may combine sentences, phrases, and words—whatever it takes to remind the speaker of what he wants to say at that point.

Notes are *reminders* to the speaker—they are not meant to be miniature manuscripts. *Notes should usually be written in outline form,* so that the relationship of ideas remains clear, and it is easy to read the notecard and still maintain good eye contact with the audience. However, the outline will be a very brief and informal one. In addition to an outline of the body of the speech, the notes may contain reminders for the introduction, transitions, and conclusion. If the notes are for a speech to be presented inductively, the ideas should be listed in the order that you wish to deliver them, even if it destroys the conventional appearance of the outline.

One question that beginning speakers have is "how many notecards should I have, and how big should they be?" Some teachers set class standards, such as one 3″ x 5″ notecard, written on only one side, which forces students to learn their material and practice eye contact. However, real-life speeches usually require more details—and more notes.

Number of Notes.   The speaker should use the minimum number of notes necessary to help him remember what he wants to say. What determines the minimum number is the complexity of the speech and the type of supporting materials used. The speaker giving the talk on Valentine's Day will need extensive notes, since it is unreasonable to memorize all the names, dates, and beliefs included in this speech.

A good example of how much information the notes should contain is the outline on diabetes in Chapter 3 (page 30). That outline indicates what the main ideas are, what will be said as the speaker moves from one point to the next, and what areas will be covered under each point. If this outline were typed single space on 3″ x 5″ notecards, it would require at least two notecards.

Size of Notes.   Notecards may be purchased in three basic sizes, 3″ x 5″, 4″ x 6″, and 5″ x 8″. If you don't wish to buy notecards, you can make your own in one of these sizes. Be sure to use heavy paper or light cardboard—regular paper isn't strong enough to withstand nervous clutches and sweaty palms.

The size of your note cards depends on three factors: the material, your handwriting, and your eyesight. If you have a long speech, large handwriting, or poor eyesight, large notecards will be more effective. The most important thing is to be able to read the notes easily so that you maintain maximum eye contact with the audience. Nothing is gained by printing super-small on a 3″ x 5″ card when a 4″ x 6″ card would be more legible. As a secondary consideration, you might think about the size of your hands—what size notecard will feel most comfortable in them?

There is one hint about putting material on notecards which you should know. If you are using an outline format, you can get more material on your notecard by turning it lengthwise (like a book), rather than by writing across it. However, if you are including many complete sentences and direct quotes, you can get more material on the card if you write across it.

There are occasions when you may wish to put notes on regular 8½″ × 11″ paper. The chief drawback to such large notes is that they are harder to handle than small ones; you should not attempt to use 8½″ × 11″ paper unless you will have a lectern so that you can keep the pages separate. A second drawback to large notes is the tendency to include more material than you have to, with the result that you read instead of maintaining eye contact.

Practicing Your Speech

In order to be truly prepared, you need to practice your speech several times before you give it. Begin practicing by reading over the complete outline so that you absorb the thoughts contained there. Then, practice delivering the speech from your notes, referring back to the complete outline if you find a spot that you're having difficulty remembering. You may need to add a few more words to the notes to help you past the spot.

Speaking from notes takes practice. The most common mistakes are:

1. Cramming too much information onto a notecard.
2. Reading the notes verbatim instead of talking about the ideas in your own words.
3. Looking at the notecards instead of the audience.
4. Fidgeting with the cards.

DELIVERY

Since the title of this chapter is "Delivering an Organized Speech," you may be surprised that it has taken this long to get to the section labeled "delivery." However, we have been talking at least indirectly about delivery in every section. Oral organizational devices—transitions, previews, and summaries—are part of the message that the speaker delivers, and speaking notes determine what kind of message he will deliver. Consequently, both topics had to be discussed before we ask the question: what can the speaker do so that he sounds organized once he is in front of the audience?

Researchers have attempted to answer part of this question, and they found that one important factor in the appearance of organization is the use of oral organization. Audiences recognize the presence or absence of transitions and rate the organization of a speech accordingly. Even if a speech is clearly structured, if a speaker forgets his oral organization, he may be rated "disorganized" by the audience.

The second important factor is whether the speaker appears prepared as he delivers his speech. The speaker who uses phrases like "now, where was I?" or "to get back to the subject" is telling his audience that he's disorganized, and they believe him—even if the structure of the speech is sound.

Thus, the delivery of an organized speech depends both on what the speaker tells the audience and on what he doesn't tell them. If you want to deliver an organized speech, make sure you do the following when standing before the audience:

1. *Act confident, even if you are not.* An audience assumes that a speaker who appears to know what he's doing is informed and organized.
2. *Speak fluently,* since hesitation is interpreted as lack of preparation, which means no organization. An organized speaker knows what he wants to say next.
3. *Don't apologize for lack of preparation.* Apologies lead an audience to expect poor organization.
4. *Use lots of oral organization devices.* Consciously think about them while you deliver the speech. Write the major organization devices on your notes, right where you want to say them, to increase the chances that you'll actually say them. Remember that they will help keep the audience with you; so don't forget them.
5. *If you suddenly discover that you have left out a point, don't emphasize your discovery to the audience, and don't fall apart.* Unless it's absolutely vital to the remainder of the speech, ignore it. If you must include it, do so calmly, explaining its relationship to what you said before and what you are going to say next.

SUMMARY

An organized speech begins with the preparation of a speech with a clear structure and an effective sequence. Once you're completed those stages, you should develop oral organization devices to help the audience perceive that clear structure and effective sequence. Prepare speaking notes that you can handle effectively while speaking, and then practice giving the speech from the notes so that you're familiar with the notes and with what you want to say in the speech. Finally, follow the rules suggested in the last section for what you should and shouldn't say while you are in front of the audience. If you do these things, you will deliver an organized speech.

11

Conclusion

The preceding chapters have examined in detail the many factors that contribute to an organized speech. This chapter sums up the elements that produce speech organization. Remember as you read them that the speaker has many alternatives in creating organized messages and that all the alternatives are not reflected in this list.

ORGANIZATION FROM BEGINNING TO END

The criteria for good organization are that the parts of the message are presented in a sequence that its listeners understand without difficulty. If you wish your speeches to meet the criteria for good organization, you should:

1. Complete the planning stage of speech preparation—analyzing the audience and occasion, choosing and narrowing the subject, and selecting the general and specific speech purposes.
2. Do some organizational preplanning—choosing a central idea and identifying a tentative set of main points.
3. Gather material for the speech.
4. Assign supporting material to the points outlined in the tentative structure; *or,* classify material to build a tentative structure.
5. Use your outline to check relationships—eliminating irrelevant material and points, and adding or revising necessary points to strengthen the speech structure.

6. Revise the structure to make the total speech responsive to the limitations imposed by time restrictions or the interests and attitudes of the audience.

7. Arrange the remaining material in effective sequences—giving consideration to the effect that the sequence will have on creating audience understanding or acceptance of your specific purpose.

8. Prepare previews, summaries, and transitions for your speech, so that the audience will perceive your organization as clearly as you do.

9. Prepare the introduction and conclusion.

10. Prepare speaking notes which are legible reminders of what you wish to say; *or,* write out a speech manuscript.

11. Practice giving the speech from the speaking notes, the full outline, or the manuscript.

12. Speak fluently while delivering the speech; be poised; make sure that you say your previews, summaries, and transitions; and be equally sure that you do not lessen the audience's confidence in your organization by apologies or other verbal slips.

13. Get some feedback on your speech, so that you'll know what you should do better next time.

The key to good organization is practice. This text has provided some, but the practice that you need most is in preparing and presenting speeches and obtaining constructive feedback. As you become more adept at implementing each of the suggestions mentioned above, you should be able to produce speeches which are increasingly well organized.

Index